Raw Materials for the Mind

Teaching & Learning
in Information &
Technology
Rich Schools

2nd Edition

By David Warlick

The Landmark Project
Raleigh, North Carolina, USA

Designations used by companies to distinguish their products are often claimed as trademarks. In all instances where The Landmark Project is aware of a claim, the product names appear in initial capital or all capital letters. Readers, however, should contact the appropriate companies for more complete information regarding trademarks and registration.

This book seeks to provide accurate and authoritative information in regard to the subject matter covered. It is sold with the understanding that the publisher is not engaged in rendering legal, accounting, or other professional service. If legal advice or other expert assistance is required, the services of a competent professional person should be sought.

ISBN 0-9667432-0-2

David F. Warlick can be reached at
919-571-3292
david@landmark-project.com

Support information for this book can be found at:
http://landmark-project.com/rmfm/customers/

Acknowledgements

This book owes its completion to a large number of people, each of whom I will not be able to thank personally on this page. I do want to express a special thank you to Paul Gilster for his continued support, suggestions, and our regular lunches, during which he teaches me about the emerging technologies that are beyond the understanding of anyone else I know. I also want to thank Al Weis for his insights and the enormous contributions of his team in bringing us ThinkQuest.

My gratitude goes out to all of the educators with whom I have worked and who have helped me to focus the ideas in this book, melding the potentials of technology with the needs of students, classrooms, and schools. Specifically, I want to thank Margaret Bingham, who taught me to think outside the box. I also want to thank the first computer visionary I ever knew, my father, who taught me how to ask questions.

Finally, eternal thanks for my wife, Brenda, for her patience, support, and especially her courage. She also performed the amazing feat of editing this book. Brenda is not on the Net, but she is in my heart.

For my children, Ryann & Martin
Future Information Builders,

My Mother, Ann Miller Warlick
Who taught me how to love,

And for
Mr. Bill Edwards
A true facilitator of learning

Contents

Introduction

I remember clearly my 9th grade civics teacher, Mrs. Cope. She was a unique teacher with a keen sense of the future -- now that I think back on it. She was the only teacher in those days who told us to pay attention to Vietnam, in a time when most of us couldn't even find the country on a map. That year, Mrs. Cope also predicted that by the year 2000, each of us would have our own computer. It would fit in our shirt pockets -- and it would add, subtract, multiply, and divide. This was absolutely incredible to my classmates and me. I had just purchased my first slide rule (if you don't remember *slide rules*, look it up) and the idea of a pocket-sized machine that would perform mathematical calculations was so far away that it didn't even rate consideration. Yet, that day I began to learn an important lesson. **What we think our civilization and its thinkers can achieve in 50 years will probably happen in ten, and what we think we can achieve in 10 will probably happen in two or three.** The past 10, 20 and 50 years have certainly borne this out.

Mrs. Cope also predicted that by the year 2000, gasoline could cost as much as 60 cents a gallon. We all vowed to ride bicycles rather than drive at that cost.

This kind of rapid and accelerating change has manifest itself in nearly every institution of our society. Computers are found at nearly every turn, from our offices, to our stores, to our homes and churches, and today, for the first time since Sputnik, we are beginning to bring education up-to-date by applying unprecedented investments in educational technology. We are selecting and purchasing powerful computer hardware, not just the low-end bargains of the past, but fast multimedia computers with CD-ROMs and network connections. As a result of corporate donations, government spending and enormous volunteer time, our schools are being wired and many are being connected to a global information network -- the Internet.

During recent months, a few people have begun to question the wisdom of such unprecedented investments in technology. They are asking, "Why?" There are several reasons.

- Part of it is momentum, urged on by the fact that virtually every other institution is rapidly becoming computerized and connected.
- It is also a technology industry that is seeking to create a market for its products and services. You only need to walk through the vendors' area of any state or national education conference to see this.
- The students are also the reason. Many believe that technology will improve student performance on standardized tests, and many studies support this belief.

Is it essential for students to be using the same technologies and applications in the classroom that their parents are using in the workplace? Is the classroom an appropriate place for giant technology industries to be fighting it out for market share? Will student performance in standardized tests continue to improve as a result of sitting at computers and will these styles of learning significantly contribute to the quality of their lives and their performance in the workplace of the 21st century? The answers to each of these questions is, "probably no!"

However, the formula is not complete. We must continue asking questions:

- Will the use of technology in our society increase in the coming years?
- Will the future hold brand new and currently unimagined technologies and applications?
- Will the amount of information that we must deal with as part of our day-to-day activities increase?
- Will the nature of what we do in our jobs be changing in the future?
- Will the nature of how we spend our leisure time change?

The answer to these questions is a resounding, "Yes," and each of these questions is brand new and unique to this day and time. As an ex-history teacher, I tend to think of issues like these in both broad and recent historical terms. I recognize, as most of you do, that we are living in one of those periods of history that is, at the same time, both exciting and tumultuous. Our day-to-day activities and concerns are changing so rapidly that it threatens many of us who hold fast to the old -- as it energizes those who ponder the possibilities.

Perhaps a useful looking glass through which to examine this time of change and its impact on our schools is how we generate and distribute our wants and needs -- our economic systems. It is largely economic systems that determine how people spend their time -- what they do from hour to hour and day to day and what skills they need to contribute to their system. This, of course, is what our schools are for, preparing our students for their future times.

Agricultural Age

A thousand years ago, many people lived and worked in an agricultural economic system. They spent their time working in the fields because the source of their wealth (their raw materials) was their cultivated fields. Out of these fields they carried crops that were largely processed in the home -- in the kitchen or at the spinning wheel. The home is also where the end products were consumed.

Raw Materials came from cultivated fields.	Raw Materials were processed in homes in the kitchen and at spinning wheels.	Processed materials were largely consumed in the home.

Industrial Age

Over a century or two, much of the world moved to an industrial economy. Quarries and forests became our source for raw materials and these materials were processed in factories. These were the places that people spent their time and did their work -- in the mines, forests, assembly lines and machine shops.

Raw Materials came from quarries & forests.	Raw Materials were moved to factories where they were processed.	Products were distributed through stores.

Information Age

We are currently moving into an information-based economic system. Here, information is the basis of wealth, and networks are the source of these information raw materials. People will spend their time accessing information from the networks, processing it into valuable information products with computers and software, and distributing their products back through the networks to information consumers.

Raw Materials come from the networks.	People process information raw materials with computer software.	Information products are distributed back through the networks.

These changes do not mean that each economic system replaces the previous one. Each new system simply changes the way that we generate our wants and needs and, perhaps even more importantly, how we spend our time as we work for our economy. When the industrial age was upon us, it didn't mean that cultivated fields disappeared. It meant that fewer people spent their time in those fields. And as the information age accelerates, it does not mean the end of factories. But it does mean that fewer people will be working in those factories, and those who do, will be doing an entirely different kind of work.

I worked in a factory for my first job out of high school. Although I was hired as a machine operator, I was quickly promoted to *setup man*, because I had taken drafting in high school and could read a blueprint. Setup men (and women) spent most of their time walking around the plan with wrenches in their hip pockets adjusting manufacturing machines, supervising operators, and looking important. But the main part of the job involved setting up the various machines. When my section had filled an order for a particular part and received a new order for a new part, my job was to read the blueprints, and then disassemble the appropriate machines and reassemble them to produce the new piece. The machines had to be constructed and aligned to drill the holes in the correct positions and depths, to mill and sand the surfaces to the precise clearances, and to perform preliminary assembly as appropriate. All of this was precisely described by paper blueprints. This workplace consisted of people who could build to specifications and many more people who could work in straight rows, performing repetitive tasks, under close supervision.

Today, the setup man is quickly becoming an icon of the past. Manufacturing is increasingly being done with software, robotics and by information technicians. People pull manufacturing specs from the network, process and translate that information into efficient instruction sets (computer programs) for the control computers, and then upload the programs back into the network where the robot machines re-purpose themselves in accordance with the newly created software.

This will require classrooms where students invent answers and construct their own knowledge within learning experiences that are crafted by creative teachers who do far less lecturing and far more facilitating and consulting.

There is an interesting characteristic about this new style of working. Because our information products are transmitted rather than transported, the setup work no long has to be done in the factory. Conceivably, I could perform this job from my basement office, or from a house on the side of a mountain in North Carolina, a beach on the coast of Mexico, or even from a high school classroom. When information becomes the key to quality production, it changes things a great deal and in unexpected ways.

One thing that it does mean is that working in straight rows, performing repetitive tasks, under close supervision, is not the style of classroom that will prepare students for their future. According to the S.C.A.N.S. report, our students will need to be creative thinking, decision-making, problem solving, analytical, self teaching, and reasoning citizens. This will require classrooms where students invent their answers and construct their own knowledge within learning experiences that are crafted by creative teachers who do far less lecturing and far more facilitating and consulting.

We will revisit this historic model later on in this book.

Technology and Schools

The First Generation

Although a few K-12 schools started using them before, computers began to appear in schools and classrooms during the early '80s as a result of what I once heard referred to as the *Kmart Effect*. It stated that only after computers began to appear in Kmart and other department stores, were they ready to be purchased for classrooms.

We have come a long way in two decades. In many classrooms today, we see students using word processors in the place of pencils. Students are using multimedia in the same way that we used textbooks and sophisticated drill & practice software for the same reasons that we used flash cards. Increasingly, students are using the global Internet to perform the same tasks that we performed with encyclopedias and other reference books.

What we have done in less than twenty years is to integrate the technology into the classroom. We have adapted computers, software, and peripherals to help us do what we have been doing for years. When presented with classrooms and the task of utilizing computers and the Internet in those classrooms, we have, in essence, wrapped the technology around the education.

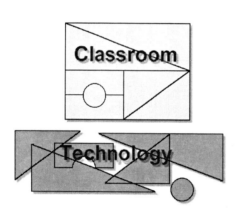 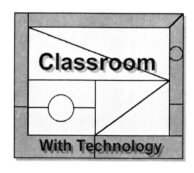

Each of the activities above represents giant leaps beyond the way that I was taught in the '50s and '60s. We know that students write better, and learn to write better with a word processor. Writing becomes a craft with this versatile tool.

Multimedia is the media of our students. Gail Morse, one of the nation's first Christa McAuliffe educators, often says that our students are light-trained, while we were paper-trained. We grew up where information was best delivered on paper. Our children, on the other hand, are growing in a world with not only pictures and words, but where video and sound abound and where increasingly we interact with the information that surrounds us in ways that put us in control of knowledge.

We know that some students learn some content and skills better with sophisticated drill & practices software. These systems track the students' performance adjusting the content and skill levels to the students' masteries and deficiencies. We also know that drill & practice is not the best application for most students. They will learn these skills with or without expensive computers and software.

The Internet and other electronic sources of information have also provided schools with unprecedented access to information in its vastness, convenience, media, and variety of perspectives.

At the same time that we recognize these technologies for their benefits we must also be aware that education is in a very critical time. While we find ourselves in a cusp between moving from industrial age education to information age education, we are also walking a fragile line between the current trend toward upgrading classrooms and a potential backlash toward more modest investments and a *Back to Basics* approach.

If sending students to the computer lab to key their reports into a word processor is called integrating technology into the curriculum, then it will fail. If having every student in the 4th grade use a comprehensive drill & practice math program is called integrating technology into the curriculum, then it will fail. If asking students to look up information on the Internet that they could more easily and quickly find in an encyclopedia is called integrating technology into the curriculum, then it will fail. We will be told that money spent on technology is being wasted and we will lose it.

While we find ourselves in a cusp between moving from industrial age education to information age education, we are also walking a fragile line between the current trend toward upgrading classrooms and a potential backlash toward more modest investments and a *Back to Basics* approach.

The Next Generation

The *Next Generation* of using computer technology in schools happens as educators begin to examine computers and the Internet to identify what is truly unique about these tools and the ways that we use them. How is the technology having significant impact on our work, on our pursuit of personal fulfillment, on our families and circles of friends? What are some of the capabilities of computers and the Internet that are less obvious to educators, but that potentially empower us to create learning experiences that were never before possible. The *Next Generation* of classroom technology will be characterized by our identifying these qualities of the technology and leveraging to facilitate more powerful learning and learning that is relevant to the inheritors of the 21st century. The *Next Generation* of classroom technology will be characterized by our adapting the classroom to take advantage of the opportunities that were never-before possible, by taking the industrial age classroom apart and then carefully and deliberately reassembling it with technology takes the places that it is uniquely qualified to take.

If the students' work can easily be done with pencil and paper, then it should be done with pencil and paper. If their work is to be compiled and published as a school literary magazine, or if it is to be e-mailed to the county commission or if images or other media are to be integrated into the work, then use a computer.

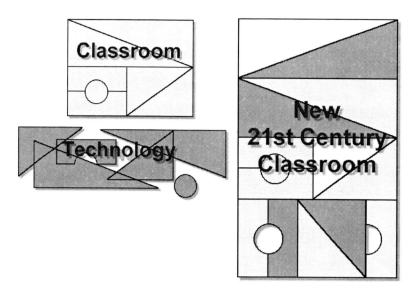

If the information is available in an encyclopedia or other reference book, then use a book. If the information or perspective that you seek is not available in the media center or if the information is to be processed in some way using a computer, then go to the

Internet. When we use technology for teaching or for learning, then we should use the technology to take advantage of its unique capabilities.

When considering the Internet, there are three qualities that are especially suited for education -- qualities that we can leverage for more powerful and relevant learning in our classrooms.

Collaboration

Students & Teachers can collaborate through the Internet with *peers, experts,* and *online communities.*

Rich & Interactive Information

Information that can be *searched, processed,* and *assembled.*

Self-Expression

Students can publish their work using *compelling media,* to *real audiences,* receiving *authentic audience feedback.*

Much of the rest of this book with examine these qualities of the Internet and related technologies. It will go into greater detail about the nature of these characteristics and how teachers can leverage collaboration, rich and interactive information, and self-expression through the Internet to create and craft brand new and powerful learning experiences.

Barriers to Creating New Learning Environments

An analogy is often described in education conferences, which is attributed to MIT's Seymour Papert. It states that if a doctor from the 1890's were to suddenly step into a hospital today, he would be completely lost. The same would be true of an office worker, farmer or most any other profession or occupation. But if a schoolteacher from the 1890's were to step into many of today's classrooms, he or she could start teaching with very little adjustment.

Fortunately, this is beginning to change, but the point is still relevant. Why have schools been so slow to change? What prevents the restructuring of our schools, while many of our industries and other institutions have been able to re-engineer their entire operations to adapt to new economic and social environments?

Two major barriers exist that are unique to schools. One is obvious to every teacher in this country, but the other is far more subtle and insidious. We'll discuss the obvious one first

Barrier One

The first barrier is mentioned in just about every education workshop that I facilitate. Teachers simply have no time to retool. There is no time left in the school day, or evening (and a surprising amount of the teacher's work is done in the evening and early morning -- on their own time) to even consider issues of restructuring their schools and classrooms.

When I ask teachers to list some of the barriers to integrating technology into their classroom instruction, lack of time is almost always the first or second one mentioned. They also mention:

- Lack of hardware and software
- Out of date hardware and software
- Lack of staff development
- Lack of technical support
- Lack of support from the administration

Teachers simply have no time to retool. There is no time left in the school day, or evening to even consider issues of restructuring their schools and classrooms.

Each of these problems will be solved. The momentum is such that we will not be able to stop the hardware and wiring. The professional development is available and much of it is good, although, many workshops are canceled because teachers lack the time to attend and most occur after the school day when teachers are tired and less receptive. Principals and other administrators are eager to bring technology into their schools and are rapidly recognizing the need for technical support. They are coming to realize that the information infrastructure is just as essential to their schools as heating and electricity.

The issue of time, however, is a more difficult one. The fact is that the workday schedule for most teachers today is practically unchanged from the teachers who taught my parents in the '30s and '40s. At the same time, the content that teachers are expected to teach has changed dramatically and so too have their students -- and this change is accelerating.

I frequently display a picture of Vera B. Hoyle in my presentations. Vera B. taught senior English to me and thousands of other students during her nearly 40 year career. She taught in a six-period day, supposedly teaching five periods and having one for planning time. Like many teachers today, she actually taught all six periods when I was in school because of rising enrollment.

Vera B. was an excellent teacher in this environment, as most of the residents of my town would agree. We would all agree because she taught us all exactly the same way and exactly the same content, from my mother-in-law to my younger brothers. She never changed, and there was very little reason to change. The tools were the same, the curriculum was the same, and the world that her students were graduating into was largely the same.

Unfortunately, if Vera B. were still teaching today, chances are that her classroom would be no different from the one that I learned in, because she would have no more time today to restructure her learning environment than she had in the '50s and '60s. In fact, she would have less time since the paperwork and added pressures of testing and accountability each eat so deeply into the school workday and teachers' creative energy.

If a giant genie from a Persian bottle were to give me one wish for education, the most far-reaching benefits would come from a restructured school day. This school day would provide for teachers a substantial amount of supported professional time for doing all of the things that teachers know are necessary for effective learning. This restructured school day would have two characteristics:

1. An eight-hour workday (teachers should be limited to only eight hours of work) from eight until five, with an hour off

for lunch. Salaries would reflect this increased time *on the job*.

2. Teachers would have one hour of planning time for each hour of teaching. In other words, half of the day would be spent in direct instructional supervision of students, and half would be spent in preparation and other activities that enhance learning.

Do lawyers spend all of their time in front of the jury? No! Do surgeons spend all of their time in the operating room? No! Do farmers spend all of their time in the fields? No! Do factory workers spend all of their time on the assembly line? Does this tell us something about teaching, about schooling, about our children?

Teachers need more time to…

- Plan lessons
- Develop teaching materials
- Create and craft learning experiences for their students
- Conduct research
- Attend professional development and engage in self-development
- Teach professional development
- Work more closely with parents and with the community
- Report to work each morning with a full night's sleep

Imagine, if every single day, teachers could bring something brand new into the classroom. Every single day, students could be challenged and motivated to learning with brand new and well-crafted experiences. Students would bring home stories about the new things that they did in school. Parents could share their stories and the image of schools would improve. The teaching profession would become much more appealing, drawing and keeping the brighter, more imaginative, and harder working professionals.

Frequently, when I suggest these ideas, people say that teachers would abuse this time. In the beginning, perhaps some would. I remember spending part of my planning period in the teacher's lounge with a soda, and with other teachers with their sodas. But I am also reminded of how you fell when you have to teach for six hours after grading papers and writing lesson plans until eleven o'clock the night before. I was reminded of this when, a few years ago, I started teaching six-hour workshops on a regular basis. When it goes well (meaning that I have spent much time planning), it energizes me. However, an hour after the session I am completely drained both physically and mentally.

Teaching requires a unique kind of energy. You are performing. You are also managing a large number of people toward goals that they do not necessarily identify with. In some classrooms it is not unlike combat, where your awareness has to be at such a refined level as to be ready to react to just about anything, because just about anything could happen.

We must take care of our teachers. Robin Little, a former state regional Teacher of the Year and current ILP and Mentor Director for Johnston County Schools, recently posted the following message on a public mailing list.

> My heart is heavy. I just told one of my first year teachers good-bye today. He has resigned and will be returning to the business world after Easter. "Sam" is (was) a lateral entry teacher who gave up a job making twice a beginning teacher's salary because he wanted to make a difference in the lives of children. He felt very strongly about this and was willing to make the time and financial sacrifices that he thought it would take to reach his goal of becoming an effective teacher. However, he did not realize how great a sacrifice teaching requires.

> "Sam" is older than many beginning teachers, is married and has 4 children. He and his wife decided that she needs to be at home with their children so he is the sole breadwinner. Since August, when he came on board with us, "Sam" has been going in debt $1,000 per month. Let me assure you that this teacher has not been recklessly spending money. They were simply trying to survive.

> "Sam" made a comment to me this morning, which I cannot get out of my mind. He said, "It's sad when our society places more value on putting cans on a shelf than on educating our children." And he would know because,

you see, Sam's previous job was as the manager of a local grocery store.*

In the 1980s, *"It was the economy, stupid!"* Today...

It's the teachers, stupid!

Barrier Two

The second, and far more subtle, barrier to school reform is societal. During the past decade, most industries and institutions have undertaken enormous change, and it continues. There is a recognition that the world is a much more fluid place than it use to be and institutions must restructure to leverage a changing world rather than just reacting to it. We must do this in order to survive and prosper.

But this restructuring has happened largely out of the public's eye. The process and price of changing offices, factories, and even government agencies has gone practically unseen by the public. The public had very little knowledge of how each of the institutions operated in the first placc, so they have not seen the particulars of restructuring. However, education is different for one very important reason. Each of us has had twelve years (more or less) of experience in K-12 classrooms. Each of us spent hours each day for years:

- Being taught by teachers who stood in front of the room,
- Completing worksheets and other assignments individually at desks arranged in straight rows,
- Speaking only to ask or answer questions,
- Consuming information to be returned at test time.

This makes all of us experts on education. This extensive experience, by its own nature, was designed to have a significant impact on our thinking, and this impact has formed an indelible

---

* Little, Robin. " Heavy Heart." Teacher of the Year Mailing List. rlittle@johnston.k12.nc.us (3 Apr. 1999).

image in our societal consciousness of what schools should do and how classrooms should operate.

This common experience is the reason why we, as parents, boards of education, and legislators react the way that we do to the perception that our classrooms are failing. We assume that classrooms are not enough like the ones in which we succeeded. If students' performance does not measure up to our expectations, then our reaction is more basics, more homework, more hours and days of instruction, and more tests. We say, "Do what was done to us -- and do it harder!"

The fact is that most parents, members of boards of education, or legislators were educated in industrial age schools when it was believed that a majority of our school mates would work industrial age jobs.

Our reliance on testing is an industrial age solution to an information age problem.

In 1973, I worked in a factory as a testing engineer. This was nothing glamorous. I used a variety of instruments to test machined parts to ensure that they were all within the tolerances described in the blueprints. In an important way, our society's increasing reliance on standardized tests is very much like my job at that factory, where we are measuring our children to make sure that they all fall within the specifications of our curriculum. Our reliance on testing is an industrial age solution to an information age problem.

Admittedly, there are basic skills, and we must assure that those skills are mastered. When I was in school, a literate citizen was one who could read instructions, fill out a job application, and calculate change. Those days are dust. The basic skills now extend to being able to work in teams, compellingly promote a position, analyze data, solve problems, and construct valuable information products.

It is now within our grasp to make the "world" our curriculum. We can virtually take students to each continent, to the planets, among the atoms of a water molecule, into interaction with other people, cooperating and collaborating toward common goals. We are rapidly entering an age where time zones are more significant boundaries than national borders or even languages.

**Yet, in many classrooms, the test
has become the curriculum!**

Flourishing will involve not what people already know but how well they can learn, adapt, solve problems, and compellingly communicate their solutions to other people. Their measure will be in their uniqueness and creativity, not in how much they are like everyone else with whom they graduated.

Our children will be working in information-based environments that are constantly changing, where their ability to adapt and add value to an endeavor will be the mark of their value to the institution. Flourishing will involve not what people already know (which is what today's tests reveal) but how well they can learn, adapt, solve problems, and compellingly communicate their solutions to other people. Their measure will be in their uniqueness and creativity, not in how much they are like everyone else with whom they graduated.

Several months ago, I was working with my 12-year-old daughter on her homework. Her English class was doing a unit on nouns. She had a study guide that listed about twelve types of nouns that she had to learn. I remembered common nouns and proper nouns from my schooling, and understood their importance (one you capitalize, and the other you don't). However, the other ten resembled nothing from my days in the 6th grade or any other grade. Although distinguishing between abstract and concrete nouns is an interesting intellectual exercise, my twenty years of speaking and writing have never required me to understand these subtle and sometimes overlapping distinctions. Yet my daughter was required to spend hours learning these definitions so that she could properly label the nouns on a test. I want to add that all things considered, I was most impressed with my daughter's English teacher. Her emphasis on writing, critical reading, and her love of the profession had earned my respect.

My son, who was 9 at the time, is not such a serious student. Although he is quite bright and makes very good grades, he would rather be doing just about anything but homework -- except perhaps piano practice. At the same time that my daughter and I were struggling over noun classifications, my son was in his room playing a video game.

He uses a very old Sega Genesis system for which it is nearly impossible to find compatible game cartridges. The only extensive source that my son has found is the local video rental store where he can rent the games for three days at a time. The problem -- or learning opportunity -- is that most of the games come without a manual. Therefore, my son must learn to play the game by diving in and exploring it. He has to discover the operation, goals, and rules from within the game and then how to use the rules to accomplish and excel in the goals.

I believe that between the two activities, my daughter's work in memorizing a classification of nouns and my son's unguided exploration of a video game, my son was developing skills that will be more relevant to his future, a future of constant change. His game playing turns out to be a very good model for their future workplace, where they will constantly be adapting to new information, new rules, new tools, and new goals. They will be successful if they learn to see the changing environment as opportunity -- it's a video game!

I am not optimistic that things will change quickly enough. One thing that I learned after nearly 25 years as an educator is that *public education is run by the public*. It is run by parents, boards of education, county commissioners, and state and federal legislatures. Very few of these people are trained educators, but they are all experts on what schools were like ten, twenty, thirty, or forty years ago. There is enormous momentum to keep schools the way that they were.

We must find a way to free our teachers to be imaginative, collaborative, and to adapt the curriculum to the real world. *We must stop forcing teachers to work harder, and start helping them to work smarter.*

Nicholas Negroponte, in his landmark book, "Being Digital," tells of a meeting that he and Seymour Papert had with Sheik Yamani at the 1981 OPEC meeting in Vienna. Negroponte explains that Yamani asked them if...

> ...we knew the difference between a primitive and an uneducated person. We were smart enough to hesitate, giving him the occasion to answer his own question, which he did very eloquently.
>
> The answer was simply that primitive people were not uneducated at all, they simply used different means to convey their knowledge from generation to generation, within a supportive and tightly knit social fabric. By contrast, he explained, an uneducated

person is a product of a modern society whose fabric
has unraveled and whose system is not supportive. [*]

The last few decades for much of the developed world has had the
appearance of an unraveling social fabric. Yet, it is with the very
circumstances that initiated the turmoil of our society that our best
hope resides. Computer technology, and the opportunities that it
offers, can become the thread with which we stitch our fabric back
together again.

By supporting good teachers with freedom, time, and tools, they
will invent new ways of teaching and learning that will be relevant
to the new world with which we are trying so hard to cope. By
collaborating beyond the classroom, learning to use the unique
qualities of Internet-based information, and providing students
with real audiences for their work we will raise the windows and
pull down the walls of our classrooms, connecting to our
community, both local and global. We will make schools a more
integral part of the communal fabric.

---

[*] Negroponte, Nicholas. "Being Digital". New York, New York: Alfred A.
Knopf, Inc., 1995.

Collaboration

If you use the Internet, then you collaborate. It is the nature of the medium. Each time you send a message or reply to one you have received; each time you share your e-mail address with a friend, associate, or an educator you met at a conference, you are opening avenues to collaboration. Throughout this book, you will see examples of how Internet tools provide links between people, links that unfold within contexts of our professional and personal goals. Within these online collaborations and resulting virtual communities, people tend to accomplish things that are bigger than any one of them.

Each time you share your e-mail address with a friend, associate, or an educator you met at a conference, you are opening avenues to collaboration.

These opportunities come at a perfect time, as teamwork becomes a growing and expected part of the workplace. Working in teams is a challenging adjustment for many of us who are already in the workplace. We were taught in traditional classrooms, where we were expected to work independently at our individual desks, purposely arranged to discourage collaboration (which was called *cheating* back then).

Giving students an opportunity to work in teams helps them to develop collaborative skills and to appreciate the value and power of combined efforts. Collaboration also helps students learn. We

have been practicing cooperative learning techniques for years and
have found that when students work together, not only do they
learn the content and skills better, but they also develop valuable
social understandings and appreciations. There are three reasons
why technology and the Internet provide uniquely powerful
opportunities to facilitate collaboration:

1. Computers and the Internet serve to combine people and
    information. In the classroom, this convergence happens
    naturally and authentically within the context of the
    curriculum. Computers and the Internet are content and
    skill machines, facilitating the exploration, manipulation
    and processing of information and the skilled construction
    of significant information products. It is a nearly perfect
    integration technology.

2. Because computers and the Internet can be used in so
    many different ways, they welcome specialization. As
    one student uses the technology to conduct research,
    another one processes the data. A third student uses the
    same machine to create graphics for the team's project
    while the forth word-processes the copy for the final
    product.

3. The Internet, through computers, begs for collaboration
    because it puts people, almost unavoidably, in contact
    with other people. Students extend their horizons to
    people and experiences beyond their physical reach.

Giving students an opportunity to work in teams helps them to
develop collaborative skills. It teaches them to respect other
people's contributions and also to value their own. When
organizing team projects, it is important to address the following
issues.

1. The assignment should be bigger than any one of the team
    members. Each person should easily recognize that they
    need contributions from each of the other members.

2. The assignment should result in the construction of a
    product. It is helpful if the product is concrete, something
    that the students can share or publish. However, this is
    not a necessity.

3. In forming teams, identify students who can learn from each other. Handicap some students. If you have a techno-savvy student working with a student who is weak in computer skills, tell the computer proficient student that she can not touch the computer…that she has to explain everything to the computer-reluctant student as he performs the search or processing.

Three Types of Collaborative Relationships

There are three types of collaborative relationships:

1. Local Collaborations,
2. Collaboration with Experts, and
3. Long Distance Collaboration

Here are some short explanations and examples of these collaborative projects.

Local Collaboration

Most classrooms have some form of local collaboration happening already. Called *Cooperative Learning*, most teachers have learned, as research has indicated, that students learn particularly well when working together. This learning often goes beyond the targeted content and skills as students develop deeper appreciation for each other regardless of, and sometime because of, their diversities.

Here are a few examples of how students might collaborate within the classroom using Internet and related technologies.

Example 1:
My children each have had to do a lighthouse project during their fourth grade year. Each student in the class had to pick one of North Carolina's lighthouses, write a report about the structure and its history, build a model, and identify a problem of their particular lighthouse with suggestions on how to address that problem.

Approached as a *Local Collaboration* project, students could be grouped, such that each team consisted of members researching different lighthouse -- no two members reporting on the same structure. They would be assigned to create a hypertext document, either a *HyperStudio* stack or a web site, that would present all of the lighthouses within some meaningful structure, i.e. geography, age, size, etc. Each lighthouse could be linked to background information that is identical in structure, requiring the students to plan together how their projects would work.

One of the advantages of using the Internet as a source of information is that the students could retrieve text, images, and even animations directly into their projects.

Example 2
One of the most important projects out of the Global SchoolHouse (http://www.gsn.org) is the *International Schools Cyberfair* project (http://www.gsn.org/cf/), which asks classes around the globe to build a web site that teaches the rest of the world something about their community. Their topics must fall into one of the following categories:

- Local Leaders
- Community Groups & Special Populations
- Businesses & Organizations
- Local Specialties
- Local Attractions (Natural & Man Made)
- Historical Landmarks
- Environmental Awareness & Issues
- Local Music & Art Forms

In constructing their web sites, students conduct research, work out strategies, plan the pages, process their information and then organize and communicate their information through the World Wide Web. All of these activities involve skills that we have been trying to help students develop for many years. As they participate in *Cyberfair*, students are developing and mastering these skills within the context of something that is meaningful to them, their families, and their community.

The most important goal of the *International Schools Cyberfair* project is to establish communication and collaboration between the classroom and their community. GSH designed the project to be a catalyst for students to work with members of their community to learn more about its heritage and goals, and to help the community learn more about what is happing in its classrooms.

International Schools Cyberfair is also a contest, and one of the most intriguing aspects of the project is the fact that the participants are also the judges. As a class registers their community web site with the project, they receive the URLs of four or five other entries along with a judging rubric. Students then evaluate these sites, taking their task as seriously as they hope other classes are taking seriously the evaluation of their project. **Assessment** is built into the project. Many teachers have reported that the evaluation process was just as valuable to their students as building their community web site.

Example 3:

Your science class is studying weather. They are also studying Africa in social studies. To integrate the two together, you and the social studies teacher decide to team up and do a unit on the characteristics of weather in Africa and how they influence the culture in each region.

From the Internet you find a map of Africa. You download the image file to disk and then make four copies of the file for each disk such that you have a disk for every two students in the class.

As the students report to class the next day, you give them their assignment. Working in teams of two, they load each of the four images of Africa into a drawing program, and use the draw features of the program to add text, lines, curves, and symbols to indicate predominant weather patterns of the continent during each of the four seasons. Then they move the images into a presentation program such that displaying the weather for each season is just a button click.

In Social Studies class, the teams will research the major regions of Africa, using a variety of resources, and then write reports on the cultures of each region -- especially how the weather of the region influences their culture. Then they will establish hyperlinks between the regions on each of the maps to the appropriate report on its culture.

Collaboration with Experts

As discussed earlier, we have all invited guest speakers into our classrooms to talk about their jobs, travel, or hobbies. The encounter is limited to one specific time and place and it tends to be one-sided in that the speaker spends all of his or her time speaking. When the Internet is utilized to bring guests into the classroom (virtually), we find that the encounter between students and guest can be extended in a variety of directions.

- No longer limited to one place and time, the encounter can be ongoing through e-mail or chat or even video conferencing.
- The guest also works with the class from his or her own environment.
- The multicasting characteristic of the Internet also allows and encourages collaboration between expert and class, making the experience more student-directed.
- Students can also work with the expert on issues that are timely, relate to the students, or are in other ways relevant to the class.

One of the most important advantages of any type of net-based collaboration is the fact that the entire correspondence is archived. The entire text of the conversations is recorded and can be issued to each participant for study and reflection, with follow-up activities planned based on conclusions that students draw.

Collaboration with experts need not be as structured as **Local Collaboration** project, though they can be. Here are a number of ideas on how students might collaborate with experts through the Internet.

Examples:

Social Studies
You might arrange a series of e-mail exchanges with a local county
commissioner, board member, or town alderman, targeting a
specific issue that is relevant to your students. The expert can
report on the process that he or she must follow in addressing the
issue and why. Then the students might return with suggestions on
how the issue might be handled from their perspective with
responses from your expert.

Science
Locate a scientist in a field that you are studying in your class,
such as astronomy. Ask the students to work together to compose
a set of four questions for the scientist that will help the class
understand their work. Then ask the scientist to explain a specific
issue that she is researching, the problems with finding the answer,
and how she and other related scientists are going about
collaborating to find the solution. Finally, ask your class to
comment back to the scientist how they think finding a solution to
the problem would impact their lives.

Literature
Find a writer. This may seem more difficult than the two experts
above, but using the techniques for finding experts, discussed in
the next section of this book, can lead to literature professors at a
local or distant colleges who might suggest writers who would be
willing to correspond with your class. It is also important to note
that all communities have writers. There are newspaper writers,
technical writers, public relations people, and many others who use
writing skills in the everyday performance of their jobs.

Just as above, the initial task is to use communication to learn
more about the work of a writer, how he goes about deciding on an
idea, developing, and putting it to paper. Students should compose
their questions in collaboration with each other to develop the
fewest number of questions that return the most information. As a
follow-up, the writer might be willing to share through e-mail part
of a piece on which he is currently working. He might ask the
students to read the work and then critique it for him over the
Internet, discussing decisions that he has made about characters,
styles of writing, and perspective.

Math
Find someone who uses math. This is easy, since it includes

virtually everyone! Good examples include accountants, programmers, inventory managers, marketing analysts, political consultants, and just about anyone else. It would even be better to identify more than one math expert and then have your students compose questions that ask each expert to explain how they use math, what problems they solve with math, and how they use computers as a math speaking tool.

Long Distance Collaboration

Increasingly, teams of people who work together on a daily basis are not located in the same geographic location. Frequently we are working across continents and around the world through e-mail, video conferencing, telephone, and groupware software. I recently collaborated with a team of educational technology specialists to create an educational CD-ROM. I worked from North Carolina, two team members worked from different towns in California, and the team leader was located near New York City. We met regularly via telephone and the web, examining and editing each others work via the web while we were simultaneously conversing over speakerphones. We were also in almost daily contact through e-mail and a mailing list.

This kind of collaborative work is going to become even more common as our endeavors become more global in nature. Students today, need to start developing skills in working collaboratively over Networks.

Example:

Perhaps the best example of this type of collaborative project is *ThinkQuest*. The brainchild of Al Weis, the president and CEO of Advanced Network & Services (http://www.advanced.org) in Armonk, New York, ThinkQuest asks students to create a web site that must be designed to help other people learn something.

The goal of the project is to establish a library of web sites that are designed explicitly as learning tools. Advanced Network & Services now has approximately 1500 projects that were, at the end of the 1998-99 school year, being accessed at a rate of 3 million hits a day. Students and teachers around the world are teaching and learning from these tools, which were built by 12 to 19 year old students, working in teams.

As engineers who have been involved in the evolution of the Internet since the beginning, the designers of ThinkQuest understood the fact that students need to learn to collaborate, and to do it over the Internet. So they made the project a contest, awarding more than a million dollars in scholarships to the students who create the best learning sites and cash for their teacher/coaches and their schools. To encourage the students to form teams from different geographic locations and between technology rich and poor schools, part of the judging is based on the degree to which the students are challenged to utilize the technology for collaboration. The idea is to challenge the students to be resourceful, understanding that innovation comes from resourcefulness.

Weis said in a June, 1999 e-mail interview, "Collaboration is not something that comes natural - especially if you have never met the other person and don't know much about them." He continued by stating,

> In the process of collaborating to build an (ThinkQuest) entry, students learn how to build a team, how to hold it together and a bit about the lives of their teammates. When students collaborate with each other over the Internet and across different cultures and time zones to create something of value and solve hard problems, they are learning an invaluable skill, a skill that will help them in their future work endeavors and their personal lives. Many are working under stress with students from different parts of the globe, and they are making life long friends - friends that one day may help them or many others in a conflicted world.[*]

The winners of the "Best of Contest" award in 1997 ($25,000 scholarships for each member of the three-member team) built an

---

[*] Weis, Al. "Re: Help with Collaboration...". (7 June 1999).

enormous web site about the Himalayan Mountains. Team
members included a 16-year-old from Georgia, a 17-year-old from
the Netherlands, and a 17-year-old from India. The students
collaborated across continents and a dozen time zones to build a
rich resource for students and teachers around the world.

> Where Earth Meets Sky: The Himalayas
> http://library.advanced.org/10131

Another example was a student from the Washington, D.C. area
who collaborated with a young woman from rural Alaska and a
boy from Russia. The problems presented by languages, time
zones, and differences in technology access were enormous. But
these students invented ways of overcoming these barriers and
created an intriguing and innovative web site about nutrition.

> You Are What You Eat
> http://library.advanced.org/11163/

You can learn more about ThinkQuest at their web site:

> http://www.thinkquest.org

Finding People on the Internet

There are essentially two types of information raw materials on the Internet, people resources and digital resources. The people resources represent the millions of people who use the global network, seeking information and contributing information to friends, acquaintances, and to broader audiences. Digital resources constitute the web pages, text, images, movie and sound files that are stored on the hard drives of web servers and other host computers on the Internet. These are files that you can access most anytime regardless of the availability of any person.

For many people, it is the people resources that attract them to the Internet. After all, e-mail is still the most often use application on the Internet. Their involvement ranges from corresponding with family and friends to joining the growing virtual communities that seem to form almost without design and with only a minimum of governance. It is breaking beyond the constraints of their geography, time, and work environment that draws them in. This need is especially true of educators, who spend most of their work time in their classrooms managing the learning of their 20, 25, or 30 students. But we will talk more about this later.

I distinguish between people and digital resources because the tools that we use to access and process these categories of information are different. For human resources, we use e-mail along with a few other specialized tools. For digital resources, we use the World Wide Web with other associated software. Much of this book describes more advanced features of both of these tool sets, features and techniques that will help make teachers and students more efficient and productive users of the Internet.

Advantages for Using People Resources from the Internet

At the same time that e-mail remains the most often used Internet application, access to people over the Internet is frequently overlooked by teachers. Clicking around the World Wide Web has a great deal of appeal. It still appears magical to many users. But even as computers become more powerful, they do not approach the computing and perceptive abilities of the human brain. Information from people tends to be:

1. **More interactive** -- people can explain things in many
    different ways. By continuing to interact with our people
    resources, asking questions, we can turn the information
    around and see it from many perspectives, appreciating it
    more fully.

2. **More dynamic** -- In this day and time, information
    changes -- almost hourly. People are highly adaptive to
    changing information, able to change the nature of the
    information they hold, perspectives, and motives.

3. **Historically rich** -- When you access information from a
    person, you can also get the history of the
    information...its roots and how it has evolved.

4. **Audience sensitive** -- People will usually attempt to share
    information on your level, in layman's terms or in
    technical language, depending on the receiver.

Finding Experts

There are a number of services on the Internet that have organized
opportunities for classrooms to collaborate with experts. Below
are some examples.

Service	URL
New Jersey Network Infrastructure in Education's Ask an Expert Page	http://njnie.dl.stevens-tech.edu/curriculum/aska.html
Pitsco's Ask an Expert Page	http://www.askanexpert.com/askanexpert/cat/
The Mad Scientist Network	http://medinfo.wustl.edu/~ysp/MSN/
The Franklin Institutes' Ask a Scientist Page	http://sln.fi.edu:80/tfi/publications/askexprt.html
Ask a Volcanologist	http://volcano.und.nodak.edu/vwdocs/ask_a.html
Ask an Astronaut	http://www.nss.org/askastro/home.html
Grammar Lady	http://grammarlady.com/

Most of these services allow the teacher or students to post a
question. The queries is then made available to a network of

experts who respond as they are uniquely qualified or because it is their week to respond to questions.

Often, you want your class to collaborate in a more engaging way than simple asking a question. This requires that you find an expert, and then negotiate an arrangement that facilitates the activity that you want for your students. The challenge here is establishing a project that is beneficial both for you and for your expert.

For instance, you are a literature teach, and your students are studying Shakespeare. The logical place to find a Shakespeare expert would be a university. You might use the technique described in the next section to locate a professor who teaches the Bard.

When you have located your expert, you want to devise some way of collaborating that would add some value to what he or she is doing as well as help your students. One idea might be to ask if some of his students would mind pretending to be the major characters of the play that your students are studying and to be available through e-mail to respond to your students' questions.

This would benefit your students, as they become more involved in the play by corresponding with the characters. It also helps the university class as its students, especially those who might be education majors, in their study of the characters of the play.

Strategies for Locating Experts in Academia

If you are looking for an expert in a particular area of interest, such as the migration of Monarch butterflies, and you do not count an entomologist among your friends, your detective work begins. A good first place to start may be the academic community. Authority is an important advantage of finding people in this way. Their universities have hired them because they are experts.

1. We will begin with a university in Mississippi, because we know that Monarchs travel through that state. First of all, we go to Mississippi's state government home page to find a listing of universities there.

The URLs for all state government resource pages are basically the same:

www.state.ms.us

…where the *ms* is the abbreviation for the state. For California, it would be

www.state.ca.us

The URLs for all state government resource pages are basically the same:

www.state.ms.us

…where the *ms* is the abbreviation for the state. For California, it would be

www.state.ca.us

2. Here I find a link to Mississippi State University. From the Mississippi State University home page, I click **Academics** and find a link to the *Department of Entomology.* Many university web pages use the term *Academics* to point toward their individual colleges and departments.

3. After I get the page for the Entomology Department, I click on **faculty** where I find experts on insect morphology, insect systematics, and insect population. Each of these faculty members has a personal home page.

4. Clicking on one of the scientists we see his picture, a list of his publications, and his e-mail address.

Strategies for Locating Experts in Government

Another authoritative source of experts is government: federal, state, and local. The level of government that you decide to use will depend on the information you seek. We have already learned that the Monarch flies through specific states, so looking at the state governments of those states would make sense.

1. First of all, we will go to the state government web site for a specific state. Remember that most states use a common URL for this resource,

www.state.mo.us,

…where *mo* refers to Missouri. You would change this to *www.state.tx.us* to load the Texas State Government web page.

2. At the Missouri state government page we find a link to the Executive Department of Conservation. There are a series of drop-down menus, one for animals of Missouri. We select **butterflies**, click **Go,** and find a fabulous page about butterflies and how to make a butterfly garden.

3. There is not an e-mail address on the butterfly page, but when we back up to the Executive Department of Conservation pages, we find an e-mail address there which is probably the address for the receptionist. Many times it is better to contact the receptionist directly, because he or she will probably have better success at getting you to the right person.

Finding Communities

The Internet has become an essential tool for scientists and other experts, especially for use in communicating with each other about their particular fields of study. In many cases, the Internet has become an online and extended conference, where specialists can discuss with large numbers of fellow experts the current issues influencing their areas of interest. One Internet tool that specialists frequently use for establishing these online discussion forums is the *Internet mailing list* -- sometimes called *listservs*. If we could join a mailing list that is used by experts in the specific area we are currently teaching, then we can tap into or eavesdrop on their conversations, perhaps learning something about the prevailing issues, problems, and interests of that field of study.

What is an Internet Mailing List?

An Internet mailing list is very similar to the postal variety. It is a list of addresses, e-mail addresses, to which messages can be sent in a bulk-mailing fashion. One person sends the message to a central e-mail address, and the message is copied to all members.

Internet mailing lists have one very important advantage over postal mailing lists. **Anyone who is on the list can send messages to the entire list of members**. Any member of the list can send announcements, solicit help, report successes and less successful projects, and open discussions. An Internet mailing list can sometimes be like an ongoing conference meeting with continuing conversations on topics of interest.

To join an Internet mailing list, you only need two pieces of information:

1. The name of the list, **List Name**.

2. The e-mail address of the computer that maintains the list, **List Address**.

Once you have this information, you simply address an e-mail message to the list address, and type in the subject of the message:

Subscribe <list name> <your name>

Then send the message. After a moment you will receive an automatic e-mail message from the computer welcoming you to the list and explaining some of the guidelines for participating in the discussions.

How do you find Internet Mailing Lists?

An excellent way to learn about mailing lists is through other mailing lists. One of the best sources for this and other types of Internet resources is *Net-Happenings*, a very old mailing list that is moderated by Gleason Sackman in Fargo, North Dakota. Sackman daily scans the Internet for new and growing Internet resources that would be of interest to educators. Then he announces these services to the teaching community through his *Net-Happenings* mailing list. To subscribe to this list, address an e-mail message to:

listserv@cs.wisc.edu

In the body of the message, type:

Subscribe NET-HAPPENINGS <your first & last name>

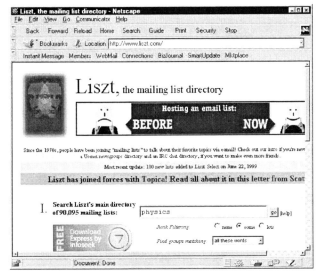

There are also a number of databases of mailing lists available on the Internet. Some of these databases are searchable. One excellent example is called *Liszt*. As an example, let's say that you are a physics teacher in your high school. To learn more about the subject, especially the current issues related to physics, you might search the *Liszt* database for mailing lists on the subject. To seek online conversations about physics, you would load the *Liszt* web page into our browser. The URL is:

http://www.liszt.com

Liszt has a search tool for finding Internet mailing lists. You type a keyword into the text box and then click **Search**. *Liszt* will list all mailing lists in its database that have the keyword in the list description or title.

You enter *physics*. If our search term included more than one word, *Liszt* can search for all of the words in our search phrase, any of the words, or the exact phrase.

The report that *Liszt* returns to us includes a number of mailing lists and seven *Liszt Select*, which have been marked by *Liszt* as especially useful and public.

II. Your search matched 7 Liszt Select lists:

astrospace-l	Discussion list for topics related to Astronomy, Space-Exploration, Astrophysics/Cosmology and SETI.
cc	Conscious Creation, metaphysics, consciousness, Seth, channeling, belief systems, and fun!
pho	Physics Olympiads
physics	"General Physics Discussion List"
ScienceThoughts	Friendly, non-technical discussions of physics.
Soulscape	Tarot, astrology, metaphysics, how-to's,
studycircle	religion spirituality comparative religion Hinduism+others Sai Baba theology metaphysics scriptures

We will click on *physics* to learn more about it.

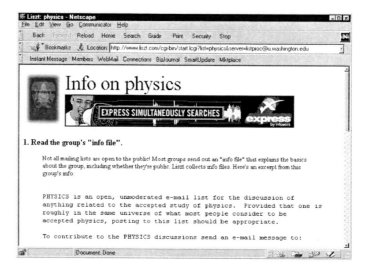

The report that *Liszt* generates includes the name of the list, a description, and other information, including the e-mail address of the computer that maintains the list. You can learn more about this mailing list by interacting with its managing computer, since list programs can accept commands via e-mail.

To get more information about *physics*, send an e-mail message to:

listproc@u.washington.edu

In the body of the message type:

info physics

A short while after sending this message, the list management program will automatically send an e-mail back to you to share what it knows about that particular list.

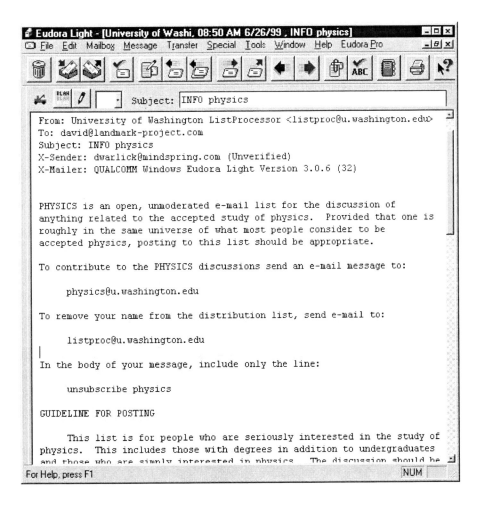

Other sources of Internet mailing lists include:

Directory Name	URL
The Directory of Scholarly E-Lists	http://n2h2.com/KOVACS/
Liszt Directory of E-mail Discussion Groups	http://www.liszt.com/
Publicly Accessible Mailing lists	http://www.neosoft.com/internet/paml/
Search the List of Lists	http://catalog.com/vivian/interest-group-search.html
EGroups	http://www.egroups.com

Some Tips for Using Mailing Lists

1. Read the e-mail message that is sent to you upon joining a mailing list very carefully. This automated message will include very important information about the purpose of the list and the types of discussions that take place there. Follow these guidelines. This message will also include instructions for removing your e-mail address from the list, should you decide to leave it.

When writing your request for information, make it short, ...the people to whom you are sending the message are busy, and do not have time to read a lengthy letter. ...keep your paragraphs short with blank lines between them. People are more likely to read this type of message.

2. Think of Internet mailing lists as forums and that they imply a sense of place for their users. You are a guest in this place and should respect its customs and wishes.

3. Most people are eager to help you. There is a genuine concern for education, and using the Internet to send valuable information to classrooms is an obvious benefit that most people appreciate. So, do not hesitate to post questions to a mailing list for your class unless it is explicitly prohibited in the guidelines posted in the introductory message.

4. At the same time that most people are eager to help education, they are also busy. They will not appreciate receiving numerous postings that do not contribute to the list's goals. So as you ask for information from experts via the mailing list, consider that this will be your only chance. Carefully word your question(s) so that you will get the most and best information for your classroom. Get your

class to help pose your questions. Learning to ask GOOD questions is an essential information age skill.

5.   Monitor the messages that are posted to the list. Very soon you will be able to identify the specific people who would be most valuable as a support for your class. Send an e-mail request for information directly to these few people. This will prevent you from adding e-mail to a multitude of mailboxes of people who would not be of help and may see your requests as an intrusion.

6.   When writing your request for information, make it short. Once again, the people to whom you are sending the message are busy and do not have time to read a lengthy letter. Also keep your paragraphs short (no more than three sentences) with a blank line between. People are more likely to read many short paragraphs than a few long ones.

7.   Use an e-mail signature to introduce yourself. Do not write a lengthy introduction in the message. Explain very briefly what your class is doing and rely on the signature to tell the readers who and where you are.

8.   If you are soliciting information from a mailing list used by K-12 educators, then promise something in return. If you are developing a new unit on butterflies, then offer to send your teacher friends a copy of the unit. If you are asking teachers to survey their students for information that your class will be compiling and analyzing, then offer to send the results of your survey to all contributing classes.

Sample message requesting information from members of a mailing list.

```
To: bugs@listserv.vm.tau.edu
From: jrobinso@wes.k12.ny.us
Subject: Info on Monarch Butterflies

Greetings,

If this message is not appropriate for this mailing list,
please disregard and accept my apologies.

A small group of students in my 7th grade science class is
doing a project on Monarch Butterflies. They want to learn
how Monarchs are able to consistently follow their
migratory paths year after year, generation after
generation.

If you can help us with an explanation or point us in the
direction of any books or web sites, they would be most
thankful.


Regards
Julia Robinson
Teacher
```

Internet Mailing List
That have Formed Professional Collaborative Communities

Net-Happenings	Send the message "sub NET-HAPPENINGS your name" to listserv@lists.internic.net
	http://scout.cs.wisc.edu/scout/net-hap/index.html
Media-L	Send the message "sub MEDIA-L your name" to listserv@bingvmb.cc.binghamton.edu
	Use of media in the classroom and in education
AltLearn	Send the message "sub ALTLEARN your name" to listserv@sjuvm.stjohns.edu
	Alternative and new approaches to education and learning
Vocnet	Send the message "sub VOCNET your name" to listserv%ucbcmsa.bitnet@listserv.net
	http://spider.ace.sait.ab.ca/academic/electric/staff/jim_murtagh/portfoli/vocnet.htm
Edpolyan	Send the message "sub EDPOLYAN your name" to listserv@asuvm.inre.asu.edu
	Education policy analysis in the U.S.
WWWEDU	Send the message "sub WWWEDU your name" to listproc@ready.cpb.org
	http://edweb.gsn.org/wwwedu.html
Hilites	Send the message "sub HILITES your name" to Majordomo@gsn.org
	http://gsn.org/majordomo/info/hilites
K12Admin	Send the message "sub K12ADMIN your name" to listserv@listserv.syr.edu
	A mailing list for K-12 administrators
LM-Net	Send the message "sub LM-NET your name" to listserv@listserv.syr.edu
	A popular and valuable mailing list for school media specialists

Professional Development Opportunities

Service & URL	Description from Their Web site
TAPPED IN **Teacher Professional** **Development Institute**	TAPPED IN™ is a growing community of over 1400 K-14 teachers, staff from several of our partner professional development organizations, and researchers engaged in a professional discourse, collaborative work, and a variety of on-line activities.
http://www.tappedin.org/	
Teachers, Technology, and the Internet	This space is now being transformed into an ongoing resource for everyone who participated in the workshop.
http://www.eecs.berkeley.edu/~maggie/Workshop/	
Best Practices in Education	BEST PRACTICES IN EDUCATION is a not-for-profit organization dedicated to working with American teachers to find effective educational practices from other countries

	to adapt and apply in United States schools.
http://www.bestpraceduc.org/	
Online Class	Are you interested in integrating the Internet into your own K-12 curriculum, but want something already organized and ready-to-go? You've come to the right place!
http://www.onlineclass.com	

Finding Peers

Locating experts over the Internet is a powerful way of accessing valuable information for your class. Locating other classes over the Internet can open up exciting opportunities for students to collaborate with each other to help them develop and master communication, information processing, and problem-solving skills.

Strategies for Finding Peers on the Internet

There are a variety of strategies that teachers can use to find classes with which to collaborate. Sometimes, the best collaborative arrangements are made between teachers who already knew each other. They may have taught in the same school at one time or met each other at an education conference. There are also opportunities to make contact with other classes over the Internet

Using Education Mailing Lists

Subscribing to an education related mailing list is an excellent way to meet other teachers with classes that might provide valuable collaborative experiences for your students. First of all, you know that these teachers already have a certain amount of technical savvy simply because they are on a mailing list. Another important advantage is that by monitoring the messages posted to the mailing list, you get to know the teachers who are most active through their ideas and contributions. You can select your collaborative classes by what the teacher has to say.

Refer back to the list of education mailing lists on page 41 for lists to join. Another source for finding mailing lists in your specific areas of education are the various education associations. Frequently, they employ mailing lists to facilitate communication among members. Here are a few education associations with the URLs of their web sites:

Organization	URL
American Association of School Librarians (AASL)	http://www.ala.org/aasl/
American Council on the Teaching of Foreign Languages (ACTFL)	http://www.rosemont.edu/flrpage18.html
American Library Association (ALA)	http://www.ala.org/

The Council For Exceptional Children	http://www.cec.sped.org/home.htm
International Society for Technology in Education (ISTE)	http://isteonline.uoregon.edu/
Music Educators National Conference (MENC)	http://www.menc.org/
National Art Education Association (NAEA)	http://www.cedarnet.org/emig/menu.html
National Association for Bilingual Education (NABE)	http://www.redmundial.com/nabe.html
National Association for Sport and Physical Education (NASPE)	http://www.aahperd.org
National Association for the Education of Young Children (NAEYC)	http://www.america-tomorrow.com/naeyc/
National Council for the Social Studies (NCSS)	http://www.ari.net/online/
National Council of Teachers of English (NCTE)	http://www.ncte.org/
National Council of Teachers of Mathematics (NCTM)	http://www.nctm.org/index.htm
National Science Teachers Association (NSTA)	http://www.nsta.org/

Using School Web Site Directories

Sometimes you would like your students to collaborate with a class in a specific geographic location. It is possible to find teachers from these places on a mailing list, but a more efficient way of locating classes by geography is to use school web directories. These are services on the Internet that allow schools to register their web sites for inclusion in the directories. There many of these directories, but perhaps the oldest and most established is Web66. The URL for Web66 is:

http://web66.umn.edu/

As an example, let's say that you are a social studies teacher, and you are preparing to teach a unit on Mediterranean culture. You would like to locate a class in Italy with which your students might create and exchange

Web66 has been around for many years. This web site was the first to suggest that schools should have their own web sites where students could showcase their work. They have a wealth of information on building and maintaining a school web site.

published travel guides for teenagers taking vacations in your respective regions. To locate such a class using Web66, you would follow these directions:

1. From the Web66 home page we click on **International Registry of Schools on the Web**.

2. The Registry of Schools is a database of schools from around the world who have registered their web site so that other people can find them.

3. A map of the United States appears. We click the word **Europe** so that we can get the Europe registry page.

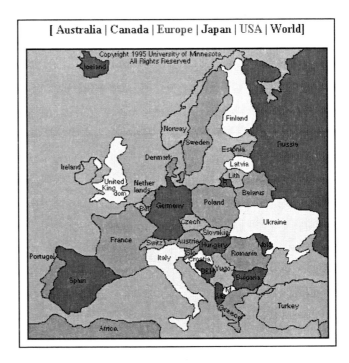

4. When the map of Europe appears, we click the outline of Italy and receive a list of elementary and secondary schools with web sites.

5. Next, you view a number of the web sites, make a record of the e-mail address of the site web masters, and then post your e-mail message to a number of them asking if they have any classes that might be interested in your project.

One of the issues that will likely occur during international collaborations is language barriers. Traditionally, languages have not been much of a problem for Internet users, since most users were from industrial countries with which English is a convenient common language. However, as more of the developing world comes online, language will increasingly become a barrier to collaborations within all communities of interest on the Internet.

To help us communicate through these barriers, several translation services have emerged on the Internet. Perhaps to most frequently used service is part of the Alta Vista search engine. The *Babelfish* service is at:

> http://babelfish.altavista.com/

When you have loaded this web page, simply type or paste the text that you would like translated into the large text box, select the language you want the text translated to, and the click the **Translate** button.

For our example, I translated…

```
Dear Teacher,

I teach 8th grade social studies in a middle
school in the United States.  We are currently
studying Mediterranean culture and would like to
establish correspondence with a class in your
country.

If you or another teacher in your school might
be interested in establishing a collaborative
project with a class in the United States,
please reply to this e-mail message.

Sincerely,

David Warlick
```

And received…

Caro Insegnante,

Insegno ad ottavo grado gli studi sociali in una scuola
centrale negli Stati Uniti. Attualmente stiamo studiando la
coltura mediterranea e vorremmo stabilire la
corrispondenza con un codice categoria nel vostro paese.

Se voi o un altro insegnante a vostra scuola poteste essere
interessati nella stabilizzazione del progetto di
collaborazione con un codice categoria negli Stati Uniti,
rispondere prego a questo messaggio di E-mail.

Francamente,

David Warlick

Now, anyone with a working knowledge of Italian will recognize
that this is far from a perfect translation. However, most of the
time it does turn what was an unintelligible message into text that
we can understand and respond to.

A couple of weeks ago, I was in a chat room with a number of
other educators. One was a teacher from Portugal who had very
poor skills in English (about as good as I am at Portuguese).
Regardless of this language barrier, we were able to converse using
Babelfish. Admittedly, the conversation was slow and clunky, but
the communication did happen where it would have been
impossible otherwise.

Peer Collaboration and Project-Based Learning

Typically, when students are collaborating with each other over the Internet, they are doing it within the context of a project. Project Base Learning (PBL) is difficult to define because it can be so many different things -- every project is different. They can be simple or they can be complex. They can involve only three or four students, your entire class, or a dozen classes from around the world. They can focus on a specific discipline, or integrate a number of subject areas.

Essentially, PBL is when students are learning skills and content by engaging in a series of logical tasks that

1. Involve the skills and content to be learned,

2. Have a personal relevance to the student(s), and

3. Provide a real-world context for the learning objectives.

Perhaps the best way to understand PBL is through an example. The following describes a project that I conducted over the Internet a couple of years ago. It was called the *Eco-Marketing Project*.

The Eco-Marketing Project

The primary learning objective of this project was to help students develop descriptive and persuasive writing skills. Students in about fifteen classes in the U.S., Canada, and Europe were divided into teams of three or four students per team. Each team became a company. Their task was to develop an imaginative new product that they had never seen in a store or shopping catalog, but a product that they thought other kids would buy. Also, at least 50% of the materials that went into the construction of their product had to be recycled materials.

After fully developing the ideas around their product, each team had to collaborate to write a sales pitch, text that not only described their product and what it did, but also convinced the reader that he or she should buy this product. After they completed their sales, each team installed the text on a web site where they became part of an on-line catalog, and other students were encouraged to come and shop. Each shopper was given 200 make-believe dollars with which they could select and mock purchase the products that they most wanted.

The writers could periodically check their product sales, another way of evaluating the quality of their writing. If they were not satisfied, they could examine the sales pitches of products that were selling, and then edit their pitch based on what they learned about writing descriptively and persuasively. Upon re-issuing their sales pitch, they could continue to evaluate their writing in terms of orders.

Components of PBL Activities

Developing project ideas for your class can be difficult. Sometimes the more simple projects can be the hardest to coordinate. At the same time that you are designing the project to help your students develop their skills, you can also add components to the project that ease your management tasks, enabling you to spend more time facilitating students' learning.

The following list may help by providing a flexible structure of sorts for your ideas. This list includes components that may or may not be present in your project idea, but each of which can add to yours and your students' experiences. I will also describe how each item is related to the *Eco-Marking Project*.

1. **Explicit connections to established instructional standards**

   The primary curriculum objective of *Eco-Marketing* was to help students develop writing skills described in the local or state curriculum standards. Additional objectives were also identified including skills and content from the science and social studies curriculum as well as mathematics and health.

2. **Collaboration either among students in your class, between students and experts, or students in a variety of classes**

   Students, first of all, were working in teams to develop and sell their imaginative product. After they had installed their sales pitches, they were collaborating with other students from across the Internet to evaluate the quality of their writing -- collaboration between producers and consumers. Another feature of this project was that students could ask questions of students in three business colleges; questions regarding marketing, supply & demand, and other issues.

3. **Information accessing, either through research or survey**

    Participating classes were encouraged to research materials to be used in their products in order to identify recycled materials that could be included in its construction. The depth of this research and its outcomes depended on the teacher. Students were also encouraged to conduct market research, testing the interest consumers might have in their product through surveys.

4. **Information processing such that students are analyzing, formatting, or assembling information -- in most cases using information processing software**

    Students could use a spreadsheet program to analyze the market research data that they collected. They also digitally assembled information into a sales pitch, using word processing software.

5. **The construction of a unique and valuable information product**

    This is perhaps the weakest component of the *Eco-Marketing Project*. Although their sales pitches were not of particular value to other people, students knew that they would be read and that other students would be making decisions about the effectiveness of their products, resulting in orders. Some of the best projects on the Internet result in information products that people actually seek out and use. *ThinkQuest*, from page 26, is an excellent example of students constructing unique and valuable information products.

6. Self assessment

This is perhaps the most difficult component to design into your project, thought it can be the most important. In the *Eco-Marketing Project*, students are encouraged to evaluate their own work and to improve it based on the student-centered outcomes...sales.

Types of Online Projects

No one has done as much thinking about online projects as has Dr. Judi Harris of the University of Texas in Austin. In 1994 and 1995, she published a column in *The Computing Teacher*, published by the International Society for Technology in Education (http://www.iste.org). In this column, called *Minding the Internet*, Judi described a structure of online instructional projects with categories that fell into one of three main genres. They were:

1. **Interpersonal Exchanges**
2. **Information Collections**
3. **Problem Solving Projects**

With Dr. Harris' permission, I am paraphrasing a number of the most commonly used project categories. You can read the complete text of her descriptions at:

http://ccwf.cc.utexas.edu/~jbharris/Virtual-Architecture/

"Keypals"

This is probably the first type of online project conducted over the Internet, and it is a frequent first leap into instructional Internet projects for many teachers. In most cases it involves individual students in one class matched up with individual students in another class, frequently in a different geographic location. The students send e-mail messages back and forth, usually on topics of their choosing.

The value of these projects is improved writing.

Research has shown that students write more, in greater detail, taking greater care with spelling, grammar, and punctuation when writing to distant audiences over the Internet (Cohen & Riel, *American Educational Research Journal*; v26 n2 p143-59 Sum 1989).

The downside of "Keypal" projects is the coordination that they require. Managing the constant exchange of e-mail with specific matches for each student in the class turns this seemingly simple project into a management challenge, making sure that each student receives his or her correspondence in a timely manner. Students frequently lose interest in the project if the exchanges are not regular and rapid.

Global Classrooms

Global Classrooms are different from "Keypal" projects in two important ways.

1. The classes communicate with each other rather than individual students
2. The communication is more structured and on topics related to the curriculum

The *North Carolina Center for International Understanding* (http://www.ga.unc.edu/NCCIU) organizes global classroom projects between rural schools in North Carolina and schools in other parts of the world. The teachers meet on-line and discuss project ideas. One issue that classes in the USA and Japan discussed was how teenagers spent their leisure time. This gave both groups of students special insights into the cultural differences and similarity between the two countries.

Electronic "Appearances"

We have all invited guest speakers into our classes to share information about their job, hobbies, or travels. The Internet provides a link with a world of guest speakers who are willing be interviewed by your class via e-mail, or even chat or video conferencing sessions. There are a number of projects on the Internet that offer experts of whom students can ask questions.

The New Jersey Network Infrastructure in Education project has a web page that links to a variety of "ask an expert" projects on the Internet. Just choose the type of expert you are looking for.

Http://njnie.dl.stevens-tech.edu/curriculum/aska.html

Impersonations

This one is fun. You have students communicating over the Internet with someone who is pretending to be someone else, or perhaps your students are impersonating another person.

Impersonation projects probably started at the University of Virginia, when educational history professor, Jennings Waggoner, "became" Thomas Jefferson over e-mail and offered himself to local elementary schools for interview through e-mail.

One of the first on-line projects that I developed was called *HistoryLink*. Fifth graders from two elementary schools drew out of a hat the names of famous people in history. Each student wrote an e-mail message to their famous person, asking them about their life and times. The messages were e-mailed to the local high school where senior English students conducted research and used a lot of imagination to pretend to be those famous people in history, answering the fifth graders' questions. Then the historic figures sent questions back asking about their contributions and how they are currently impacting on today's society.

Virtual Gatherings

Virtual gatherings are characterized by students gathering from different geographic locations at a specific cyber location in real time. Frequently this is done through chat rooms or video/audio conferences. Perhaps the best example of virtual gathers is when students meet in a Multi-User

Domain (MUD). MUDs are text-based virtual realities where visitors read about their surroundings, moving from room to room and manipulating objects by typing two or three word commands. From inside a MUD, students can also communicate with each other within the context of a place. Students can also collaborate in building objects and places in the MUD, such as a 15th century Danish castle while studying Shakespeare.

Information Exchange

These are typically very simple but powerful projects that involve students sharing information with each other over the Internet. Usually, they involve a web-based or e-mailed survey that seeks information related to a topic the class is studying.

Dr. Harris describes one of my projects as an example of Information Exchanges, a project called the *Global Grocery List*. This project involves a web form that asks students to record the average price for each item in a standard grocery list. The list also includes the price of gasoline, housing costs, and per capita income -- as well as the map coordinates of the students' location. The data is compiled on the *Global Grocery List* web site (http://landmark-project.com/ggl.html) where classes can download it and use the information in a variety of classes including social studies, science, mathematics, home economics, and others.

Finding Existing Online Projects

The best way to start using Project Based Learning in your classroom is to participant in a project that has already been developed. There are a variety of web sites that host or list online projects. Here are just a few:

Site Name	URL
Global SchoolHouse	http://www.globalschoolhouse.org/
IEARN	http://www.iearn.org/iearn/

Pitsco's Launch to Online Collaborative Projects	http://www.pitsco.inter.net/p/eollab.html
Houghton Mifflin Company Project Watch	http://eduplace.com/projects/index.html
TEAMS Classroom Projects	http://teams.lacoe.edu/documentation/projects/projects.html#current
KIDLINK Special Projects	http://www.kidlink.org/KIDPROJ/
The Learning Space	http://wearningspace.org/global_conn/list/projects.html
TENET	http://new-database.tenet.edu:8101/tnp-owa/tn.main.pg
EnviroNet	http://earth.simmons.edu/
Blue Web'n	http://www.kn.pacbell.com/wired/bluewebn/
The WebQuest Page	ttp://edweb.sdsu.edu/webquest/webquest.html

Perhaps the most valuable resource on the Internet for finding and announcing online projects is Global School House's *Projects Registry*. The *Projects Registry* is an online database of projects that have been developed and implemented by teachers from around the world. Here you can search for projects for your class by subject area or grade level. You can also post your own project to the database for others to find as a way of soliciting collaboration from other classes. When a project has been posted, it becomes part of the databases, but it also is forwarded into a number of education related mailing lists. As a result, your project lands into the e-mail boxes of teachers around the globe within 24 hours of your submitting it. The *Projects Registry* can be found at:

http://www.gsn.org/pr/

Developing & Publishing Your Own Online Projects

Dozens of online projects are announced on the Internet every day, and each one is different. There are templates available to help you structure your proposal, and you should use them. But do a whole lot of thinking and planning first.

Here are some steps that you will likely move through during the development and implementation of the project:

1. Identify a need. What is the problem that you want to solve? What instructional goals or objectives do you think could be more effectively learned by your students by participating in your on-line project?

    a. Are the goals or objectives that you want to achieve part of your state or local curriculum standards?

    b. Are the goals or objectives measurable?

    c. Are the goals or objectives common so that your project will be appealing to other teachers, potential collaborators?

2. Inventory the hardware, software, infrastructure, and skills that you have along with the staff that is available to you.

    a. Do you have access to computers that can run web browsers, e-mail and other communication programs?

    b. Do you have access to the software that you and your students will need to achieve the type of communication that you would like?

    c. Is your infrastructure such that your students can accomplish the communication that you would like and is the infrastructure reliable enough that other classes can depend on your project?

3. Design the project. The best approach to take in designing your project is to work backward.

    a. What do you want students to be able to do or know as a result of the project?

    b. What actions by the students will help them develop the target skill or knowledge?

    c. How could those actions be aligned with real-world applications? How can you add relevance to what the students will be doing?

    d. In what ways can you integrate what the students would be doing with other goals or objectives and other disciplines?

    e. How will the project work? Remember the components of online projects from earlier in the book, and remember that not all projects must have all components, but each adds dimension and richness to the students' experience.

> Note: Make every effort to economize your project. Find ways to automate the management as much as possible. Every minute that you are spending managing the project is a minute that your students are without your consulting.

4. Design a strategy for evaluation.

   a. How will you measure the success of your project?

   b. How can you design the performance measurement into the course of the project?

5. Write a project proposal. Once again, there are a number of templates available on the Internet for writing project proposals.

   How to Design a Successful Project
   by Yvonne Andres & Al Rogers
   http://www.gsn.org/teach/articles/design.project.html

   Telecommunications in the Classroom: Keys to Successful Telecomputing
   by Al Rogers, Yvonne Andres, Tom Clauset, and Pam Jack
   http://www.gsn.org/teach/articles/keys.2.success.html

6. Promote your project.

   a. Look for mailing lists, newsgroups, and web forums that cater to the types of teachers who would be interested in participating in your project.

   b. Register your project on the Global School House *Projects Registry* (http://www.gsn.org/pr/).

   c. If you are going to a conference or other meeting where potential participating teachers might be found, draw up a flyer to pass out. Take great care in designing your flyer. Include the instructional objectives, the highlights of what the students will be doing, and the final outcome. Also take a picture of your class, digitize it and include it on the flyer. Most importantly, make your contact information as clear as possible.

You've dropped your hook and worm into the water. Now wait for a bite.

Tools for Collaborating over the Internet

Address Groups

Most e-mail programs have the capability of establishing address groups. Typically this is a single e-mail address that represents a list of other addresses, such that you can address a single message to the representative address and have it copied to the entire list of addresses. This makes a very effective way of communicating with a team of teachers who are involved in a specific project. Here are instructions for establishing *address groups* with Eudora and Netscape's Messenger programs.

Instructions for Setting Up Group Message Addresses	
QualComm Eudora http://www.eudora.com	1. Pull down the **Tools** menu and select **Address Book**. 2. On the address book dialog box, click the **New** button. 3. Enter a name for the address group. 4. In the address box, enter the e-mail addresses of the people to be added to the group. Separate each message with a carriage return. 5. Close the address book dialog box. 6. A prompt will ask if you want to *Save changes to the address book?* Click **Yes**.

Netscape Messenger http://www.netscape.com	1. First, make sure that all members of the list have already been added to your address book. 2. Pull down the **Communicator** menu and select **Address Book**. 3. On the address book dialog box, click the **New List** button. 4. Enter the List Name, List Nickname, and a Description. 5. Arrange the mailing list window so that you can see it and the address book window at the same time. 6. Find the first person that you want to add to the list from the address book. Grab the address icon with the mouse and drag it into the mailing list window. This will add his or her e-mail address to the list. 7. Continue until all members have been added.

Establishing Your own Internet Mailing List

One of the oldest tools for collaborating over the Internet is still one of the most valuable -- Internet Mailing Lists (listservs). Traditionally, establishing a mailing list required having access to an Internet host computer, list management software, and a certain amount of techno-savvy to be able to run the software. Today, however, there are a number of web-based mailing list services that give any Internet user the ability to establish and manage sophisticated mailing lists with a number of valuable features. They include, but are not limited to:

Service	URL
ListBot	http://www.listbot.com/free.html
OneList	http://www.onelist.com/
EGroups	http://www.egroups.com

* Most of these services involve discreet advertising for income.

EGroups is an especially powerful service. It provides a wide variety of set up parameters allowing you to customize your list in a number of ways. As an example, let's say that you are a social studies teacher, and you would like for your students to learn more about their local heritage. To accomplish this you have chosen to create a mailing list that includes your students and a number of local history experts. The following is the procedure for setting up such a mailing list:

1. Establish an account with EGroups -- go to the web site (http://www.egroups.com) and click **Join for Free!**

    After you enter your e-mail address on the next page and click continue, you will receive an e-mail message with a validation number. Use this number on the form that appears on the next web page. You will be asked to enter the:

    - Validation Number,

    - Your name,

    - Zip code and country, and

    - A password

    You will return to the login page where you enter your e-mail address and password. If your browser is set up to accept cookies, then you will not be required to login on your next visit, unless you explicitly logout.

2. To start a new mailing list (or e-group), click **Start eGroup**. You will receive a form for customizing your mailing list, similar to the one on the next page.

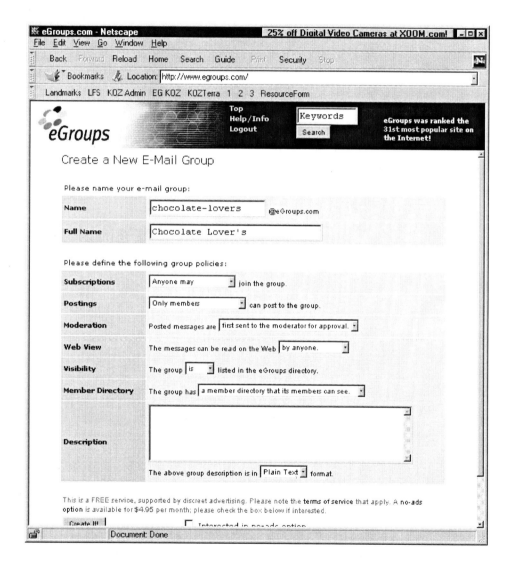

The options on this form enable you to set your mailing list for your specific needs

Name --

This is a short abbreviated name for your mailing list. It will serve as the e-mail address that people will use to post messages to the list. If you choose *townhistory* as the abbreviated name of your list, then your students and the town historians will address their messages to: townhistory@egroups.com

Full Name --

This is a more descriptive name for your list. If you abbreviated name is *townhistory*, then a full name might be *Discussing our Local History*.

Subscriptions --

This drop down menu provides two options:
1. **Anyone May**
   If this option is selected, then anyone can join your mailing list by sending the appropriate e-mail or by visiting the eGroups web site. This would probably not be the best setting for our *townhistory* mailing list
2. **Approval is required**
   If this option is selected then you would be notified if anyone tries to subscribe to the list. You will receive notification by e-mail and will be able to accept or reject the subscription by replying to specific e-mail addresses.

Postings --

This drop down menu provides three options:
1. **Only members**
   This option means that only group members can post to the list. This would be the appropriate setting for our *townhistory* list.
2. **Only the group moderator**
   This means that only the group moderator, you, can post to the list. This setting is used if you are building your list to publish an e-mail newsletter or an announcement service.
3. **Anyone**

If this option is selected, then anyone can post to the list. This is a setting that should be used cautiously and with good reason.

Moderation --   This drop down menu provides two options:
1. **Distributed directly to the group**
    This means that as members send messages to the list, each member will automatically receive a copy. This would most likely be the setting for your *townhistory* list, unless you suspect that students might abuse the messaging.
2. **First sent to the moderator for approval**
    This option means that all messages sent to the list will first be e-mailed to the list moderator. This setting would enable you to monitor and screen out all inappropriate messages.

Web View --   EGroups can archive all of the messages from your mailing list onto a web page. They can be sorted by author, date, or by subject. You may or may not want casual visitors to the eGroups web site to be able to see the messages. Your options are:
1. **by anyone**
    Anyone can read the messages.
2. **by members only**
    Only members can view the messages from the web archive.

Visibility --   Each eGroup can have a web page where a description can be read as well as the archived messages. You select either *is* or *is not* visible on the eGroups master directory. You would probably set your *townhistory* list so that it is not visible to the casual visitor.

Member Directory --   A directory of list members can also be viewed on your eGroup web page. However, casual visitors to eGroups can not see this list. This setting indicates whether you want list members to see the directory. Your options are:
1. **A member directory that its members can see**
    This would produce a directory of members that only the members can see.
2. **No member directory, not even for its members**

This would hide the members directory from everyone except the list administrator.

Description -- This should be a clear paragraph or two that describes the purpose of the list, the kinds of issues to be discussed and any specifics for the intended audience. This description will be read by other people who are considering joining your online community.

3. After you click the **Create it** button, you will get a form with two large text boxes. In the first one, enter the e-mail addresses of your students and the local historians. You can enter any number of e-mail addresses, but each one should be separated by a **<Return>** key. Beneath that box you can select whether you want to subscribe the people directly or for them to be invited to join. If they are invited to join, then they receive an e-mail message describing the list. They can join the list simply by replying to the message.

4. In the next large text box type a message that will either invite members or simply describe the list to people who are being subscribed directly.

5. Click **Add Subscribe/Finish Setup**. The next page will include some HTML code that you can add to any web page that you have on the Internet. The code will produce a small form through which you can invite people to enter their e-mail address to join your mailing list. The form will look like this.

One of the most important features of eGroups mailing lists is the web site that is established for your list. Here is a screen shot of a site for NCWebsters, a mailing list for school and school district web masters in North Carolina. Included are some notes and the various features of this site.

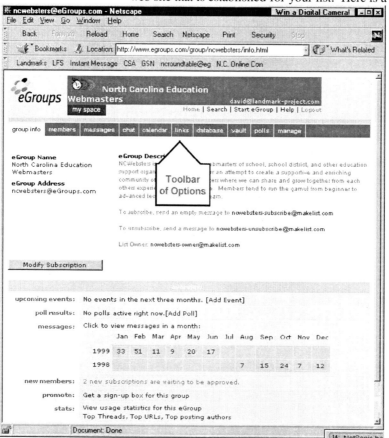

The toolbar options include:

Group Info	This is the page that you see above. It includes a description of the list, a table that indicates the amount of traffic (number of messages) in the list and other information.
Members	This tool presents a directory of the list members. List members can fill out a form with their profile

	information that will be available to all other list members. This, however, is strictly voluntary.
Messages	Clicking this tool button will produce a list of all messages posted to the list. The messages can be sorted by author, date, or subject. A recent feature enables the messages to be sorted by subject thread, meaning that all messages that are related to a specific topic will be listed together.
Chat	EGroups now has a chat room that is available only to list members.
Calendar	The calendar feature enables members of the list to post events that are relevant to the topic of the list. Events that are added to the calendar can be automatically announced to all members through e-mail.
Links	This feature enables list members to contribute to a list of web sites relevant to the topic of the list.
Database	The database page will hold data sets installed by list members.
Vault	The vault will hold files such as word processing, image, movie, and other types of information.
Polls	List members can post single question polls through the web site, electing to have the results tallied on-going or at the end of the survey.
Manage	This provides a variety of tools for the list administrator for managing the messages and members.

Here are some example school applications for mailing lists:

1.   School Committees

2.   Teacher collaborators in an instruction project

3. Parents of your students for announcements or home
    assignments

4. Other teachers of your subject within your school system

5. Students from difference geographic locations

6. Student clubs

Establishing your own Internet Chat Room

Chat rooms are immensely popular with school-aged children.
They make friends, cut up, talk about their homework, their
friends, parents, etc. Chat rooms do have a reputation as being one
of the least safe realms of the Internet, a result more of media focus
than a high number of actual instances. For this reason, chat rooms
have not been eagerly utilized by teachers, and some school
districts have essentially outlawed their use.

The fact of the matter is that teachers can now establish chat rooms
for their classes that become secure environments within which
students can safely interact with other students, teachers, or
experts. Is there any value in asking students to enter a chat room
and talk about their studies? Here are some possible benefits:

1. Improved comprehension of the content as students are
    required to interact with the information that is being
    displayed on the screen.

2. Improved verbal communication since students receive
    immediate and constant feedback from peers on their
    ideas as they interact with each other.

3. Improved reading rate, since success in this appealing
    environment depends on keeping up with the
    conversation.

4. Improved keyboarding skills since success depends on
    communicating your ideas efficiently.

5. Post chat reference material since the entire chat session
    can be logged and a transcript printed.

Here are several services on the Internet that enable you to
establish chat portals through your school or classroom web page.

Service	URL
IRC.Ramlink.Net	http://irc.ram-page.com/
CrZyChat	http://ww.crzy.com/
MultiChat	http://www.multisoftcorp.com/
SneakerChat.com	http://sneakerchat.com/
ParaChat	http://www.parachat.com/
Beseen.com	http://beseen.com/

Setting up a CrZyChat Room off of your School or Classroom Web Site

How does this work?

When you visit the CrZyChat web site, they generate some HTML
code along with some JAVA script that you then copy into your
clip board and then paste into the code for a web page that you
create. This enables you to include text on the chat page including
learning objectives, guidelines, netiquette items, and others.

Through this portal, you will be able to visit other chat rooms.
However, you will likely want to establish and register your own
chat room for your students, and set it up with the desired security.
You will also be able to customize code that you get from
CrZyChat to send your students directly to your chat room.

Here are the steps that you follow:

1. To get your CrZyChat code, go to:

    http://www.crzy.com/

2. Next, press the link for **Register for Free**. This will
    provide a list of options.

3. Click the first option, **Get/Upgrade your free CrZyChat
    Room**.

4. Type in your e-mail address and the URL of your class or
    school web site. Then click **Go**.

5. You will receive a web page with two sets of code to copy and paste. Choose the top code. Highlight it, copy it, and then paste the code into the right position on your page code.

6. Create a name for your room. It should be descriptive and include references to education or learning -- *John's-Virtual-Classroom*. Somewhere within the CrZyChat code you will find the words, *#Trial-Room*. Replace it with a # and your chat room name -- *#John's-Virtual-Classroom*.

7. Upload the page to your web server, pull it up into your browser and begin.

You will find yourself in the chat room. Now you need to register the room so that you can make it secure.

1. Click the **Cmd** button in the lower right corner of the window. Then click **Room Options**.

2. In the window that appears, click **Register**. Then click the **Room Options** tab and consider the following settings.

    Secret -- This will make your room invisible to other users of CrZyChat.

    Strict Moderation -- Chatters will only be able to speak when you give them permission.

    Invite Only -- People can only enter the room if they are invited.

The chat windows and options will look like this!

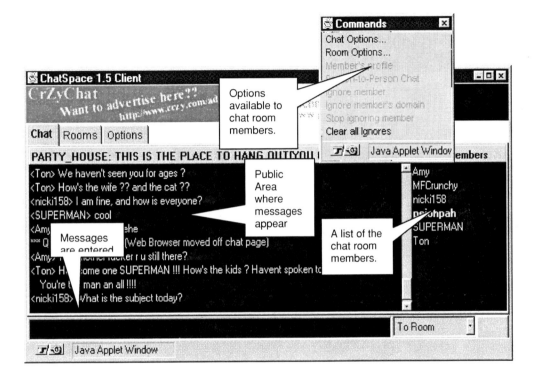

An Alternative to Chat Rooms

There is a brand new genre of software called *Chat Messengers*. They are very much like chat programs, except that they do not involved the use of a chat room. You link with other people or groups of people out on the Internet who are also running the software. There are two important benefits to using these new programs:

- One of the benefits is the security. Since your teams of students in your classroom are not visiting a room that other people might happen into, they are not likely to have interruptions from uninvited guests.

- Another advantage is the additional tools that come with Chat Messengers. Some feature file transfer so that as you or your students are collaborating with another team in another part of the world, they can transfer work files back and forth. Another feature that some Chat Messengers offer is whiteboards so that members of the chat session can collaborate by drawing on a common graphics board.

Here are a few Chat Messenger programs:

Service	URL	Platform
AOL Instant Messenger	http://www.aol.com	Mac Win
ICQ	http://www.icq.com	Mac Win
PeopleLink	http://www.peoplelink.com	Mac Win
PowWow	http://www.tribal.com	Win

Here are the standard PowWow chat window and whiteboard.

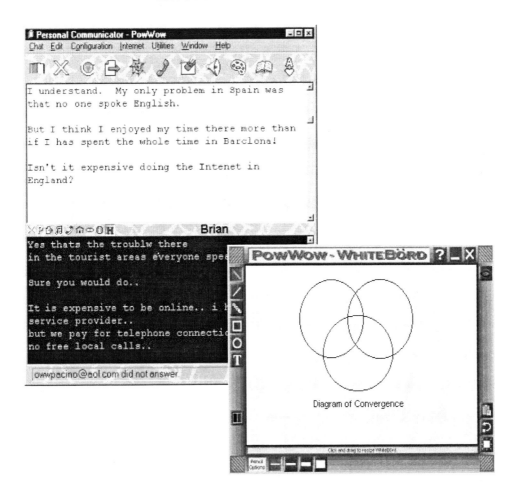

Establishing a Video/Audio Conference for Collaboration

The Internet has been a historic phenomenon, and in large part owes its success to the fact that it so effectively communicates text and images around the globe. To a less effective degree, it communicates video and audio. However, the Internet will reach its ultimate pinnacle when we can communicate seamlessly face-to-face from anywhere over this network.

This is beginning to be a reality in many classrooms. Here is what you need:

Hardware	
•	Computer (Windows or MacOS), connected to the Internet. The faster the connection, the better the quality of video and audio.
•	A Camera for projecting your image. Some examples include:
	• The Vizcam by Canon -- approximately $995
	• The QuickCam from Logitech -- approximately $79
	• The E-Cam -- approximately $79

Software	CU-SeeMe -- Commercially available at White Pine
	▪ http://www.wpine.com/
	Cornell version available for free at:
	MacOS
	▪ http://www.cu-seeme.net/release/
	▪ ftp://gated.cornell.edu/pub/video/html/get_cuseeme.html
	Win 3.x
	▪ ftp://papa.indstate.edu/winsock-l/VideoConferencing/CU-SeeMe/cuseeme.zip
	▪ ftp://papa.indstate.edu/winsock-l/VideoConferencing/CU-SeeMe/cuseeme.zip

Win 95

- ftp://papa.indstate.edu/winsock-l/Windows95/VideoConferencing/cu-seeme.zip
- ftp://gated.cornell.edu/pub/video/Win32/cu-seeme.zip

A Place to Meet People

In the same way that people meet at chat rooms when chatting, video conferencing typically requires a common place to meet on the Internet. For CU-SeeMe, the place is called a *Reflector*. The Global SchoolNet Foundation has a list of upcoming education-related video conferencing events with their *Reflector* sites. GSN also has a list of schools on the Internet who use CU-SeeMe

The schedule of events is at:

http://www.gsn.org/cu/calendar.html

The list of Schools is at:

http://www.gsn.org/cu/_cfm/countrylist.cfm

Using your video camera and CU-SeeMe are remarkable simple:

1. Install your camera as described in the user manual.

2. Download the software from one of the sites above, then install it.

3. Run the software.

4. Pull down the **View** menu and select **Preferences**. Then enter your name or a handle for **Your Name**.

5. Pull down the **Conference** menu and select **Connect**. If the conference you are entering requires an ID number, enter it as well. Then click **OK**.

6. After a moment, windows should start appearing with faces in them. If your computer has a microphone, you will be able to talk with the people you see. If you do not have a microphone, or if you are connecting to the Internet through a modem, it may be easier to use the chat feature of CU-SeeMe. To activate the chat window, pull

down the **View** menu and select **Chat**. You will receive a standard chat window.

Here is a screen shot of a CU-SeeMe session using the freeware Cornell version of the program

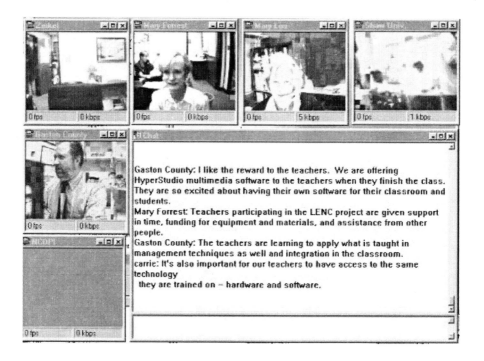

Teachers Connect, a project of the North Carolina State Department of Public Instruction, has begun to realize the potentials of videoconferencing as a distance learning tool. Through a feature, called *Town Meetings,* they offer a monthly online session with master teachers and consultants with the State Department of Public Instruction on a wide variety of topics, including:

- Assessment/Evaluation of Web sites,
- Team Teaching and Collegiality,
- How to Get the Most from Search Engines,
- Visions of Technology in Education,

- The Safety Nets of Inclusion,

- Technology and Re-structuring Schools, and

- Mentoring and Teacher Portfolio Assessment.

Dr. Mike Ward, the State Superintendent of Public Instruction, met with teachers in North Carolina through a CU-SeeMe Town Meeting.

Because of the limited bandwidth of most schools in North Carolina, *Teachers Connect* has offered these interactive sessions as CU-SeeMe video, but utilized a chat feature for the communication rather than audio. One advantage of this arrangement is that they have been able to archive the full text of each of their sessions. You can review these sessions at:

http://www.ofps.dpi.state.nc.us/OFPS/tc/town/cuarchiv.htm

E-mail Tech Tips

Organizing E-mail

As educators increasing rely on e-mail for communicating with associates, it becomes more important to keep e-mail messages organized especially as volume grows. For instance, it may become useful for a teacher to keep e-mail messages from parents together in one place, and message from administration together, or messages related to specific projects sorted together.

Most e-mail programs facilitate this sort of organizing by enabling users to establish separate folders or mailboxes for specific categories of messages. The teacher could create mailboxes each for parent correspondence, e-mail conversations with administrators, and communications related to specific projects.

Establishing Mailboxes or Folders for Organizing Messages

QualComm
Eudora
http://www.eudora.com

1. Pull down the **Mailbox** menu and select **New**.

2. Enter the name of the new mailbox. It should be short but easily recognized for the type of messages stored there. If you are making a folder, within which a specific category of mailboxes are being stored, click the **Make it a folder** checkbox.

3. With *Eudora*, mailboxes are always listed to the left of the main work area. To move a message from the **In** box to the appropriate mail box, drag the message icon into the target mailbox.

4. To open and view the messages of a specific mailbox, double click the mailbox icon. It will open a window listing the messages. You can sort the messages by sender, date, or subject by clicking the column heading.

Netscape
Messenger
http://www.netscape.com

1. Pull down the **File** menu and select **New Folder**.

2. Type the name of the folder.

3. Select an existing folder within which to store your new folder. If you are unsure, select the **Inbox**.

4. To see all message folders, click the **Discussion Groups** icon in the lower right corner of the Netscape Messenger window.

5. To move a message from the **Inbox** to its appropriate folder, drag the message icon into the target folder icon.

6. To open and view the messages of a specific folder, double click the folder icon. A list of messages will appear in the message list window. You can sort the list by subject, recipient, or date by clicking the column heading.

E-mail Tech Tip

Filtering Messages

As the daily volume of e-mail increases, it becomes impossible for teachers to find the time to manage it all. Many of the messages do not need to be read, but simply filed away to the appropriate mailbox or forwarded to the appropriate person.

Most e-mail programs have the ability to automate various tasks with e-mail messages, examining the message for specific characteristics and then processing the message as described, moving it into the correct mailbox or folder, passing it on to an associate, or deleting it. This feature is usually called a filter or a rule.

Here are instructions for setting up e-mail filters.

Establishing Filters for Automatically Acting upon Incoming Messages

Note: To establish a filter, you must identify a characteristic that all messages to be addressed by your filter have in common. For instance, we'll say that all messages are from the e-mail address *net-happenings@listserv.wsc.edu* are to be moved into the **Net-Happenings** mail box or folder.

**QualComm
Eudora**
http://www.eudora.com

1. Pull down the **Tools** menu and select **Filters**.
2. Click the **New** button in the lower left hand corner of the filters window.
3. Starting at the top of the filter dialog box, click the **Incoming**, **Outgoing**, or **Manual** checkboxes.
    a. Incoming -- Acts on messages that have been addressed to you from the Internet. This might include all messages from a specific Internet mailing list.
    b. Outgoing -- Acts on messages that you address to other people. This might include all messages addressed to your principal or to any parents.
    c. Manual -- Acts only when you pull down the **Special** menu and select **Filter Messages**.
4. Pull down the **Heading** menu in the filters dialog box and select **From**. *(see the note above)*
5. Pull down the menu that defaults to **Contains**. This menu features a number of conditions including **is**, **is not**, **starts with**, **does not start with**, etc. Select **Contains** for our example.
6. In the field to the right of the **Conditions** menu, type:
    net-happenings@listserv.wsc.edu
7. If there were other conditions to check for, you would pull down the menu that defaults to **Ignore** and select the appropriate connector, **and**, **or**, or **unless**. For this example will leave it at **Ignore**.
8. Pull down the first **Action** menu and select **Transfer to**. Then pull down the menu that appears to select the **Net-Happenings** mailbox.

Establishing Filters for Automatically Acting upon Incoming Messages

Note: To establish a filter, you must identify a characteristic that all messages to be addressed by your filter have in common. For the sake of this example, we'll say that all messages are from the e-mail address *net-happenings@listserv.wsc.edu* and that we want all of these messages moved into the **Net-Happenings** mail box or folder.

Netscape Messenger
http://www.netscape.com

1. Pull down the **Edit** menu and select **Message Filters**.
2. Click the **New** button.
3. Type in a name for the filter. In this case *(see the note above)* we might call the filter *net-happenings*.
4. The description of the filter is conversational. It says, "If the **[Part of the Header]** of the message **[Condition] [Text]**, then **[Perform Action] [Place]**."
5. From the **Part of the Header** menu, select **sender**.
6. From the **Condition** menu, select **contains**.
7. In the text box, type: *net-happenings@listserv.wsc.edu*
8. If there are other characteristics to test for, click the **More** button. This will produce a second sentence for testing.
9. From the **Perform Action** menu, select **Move to folder**.
10. From the **Place** menu, select **Net-Happenings**, a folder you have already established.
11. Click the **Filter On** and then click **OK**.
12. After this is done, all incoming messages that are from net-happenings@listserv.wsc.edu will automatically be moved to the **Net-Happenings** folder.

Multi-User Domains (MUDs) -- for the truly adventurous

Multi-User Domains are weird and definitely not for everyone. But they hold a great deal of potential for helping students improve their writing, reading, problem-solving skills, and content knowledge.

To understand MUDs, you have to think back to the old days -- before graphics. You booted up a disk in your Apple II and immediately saw a text description of a place. It might read:

> You are in a wood-paneled room with several portraits hanging from the wall, two comfortable leather chairs, and a walnut desk. On top of the desk is a diary. There is a single drawer in the desk. There is a door to the north and a door to the south.

From this description, you would type in two or three word commands such as:

Open drawer

Read diary

Look down

Go north

Go south

If you type in, "go north," you might read:

You walk through classic French doors into a comfortable patio. The sound of a fountain accents the sense of relaxation. There is a Mediterranean style iron table with a glass top and similarly styled chairs. You see an envelope on the table with a name elegantly penned in calligraphy.

You would continue to move from place to place, examining the objects that you find, all within the context of solving a crime, hunting down a vampire, or some other fantasy goal.

MUDs work exactly the same way, except that they exist on the Internet. You use special MUD client software to connect to a MUD server where you immediately read the description of where you are. One of the major differences between MUDs and the old adventure games is that if another person is using your MUD from somewhere else on the Internet, and they are in the same room as you, then that person becomes part of the room's landscape. Not only do they become part of the environment, but you can communicate with that person.

If I type:

"Hi, John, how are you doing?

John would read:

David says, "Hi, John, how are you doing?"

Then when John types:

"I'm doing fine, Dave, how are you?

I would read:

John says, "I'm doing fine, Dave, how are you?

I could then reply, expressing my elation at being here:

:turns two backward flips.

John would read:

David turns two backward flips.

This, of course, is a thrill for a 47-year-old.

By conversing through speech (typing), gestures, and within an environment; far richer communication can take place than with standard chat services. Here is a standard MUD Client program Window:

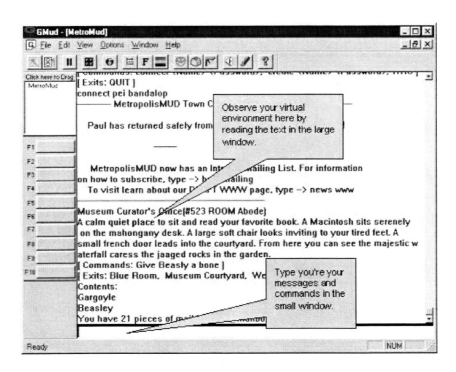

Another element of MUDs is the fact that you establish an identity for yourself, so that as other people look at you, they read a description, which you have set for yourself. For instance, instead of seeing an ungracefully aging computer consultant, my MUD friends see...

…Pei-Oh-Pah, a tall, lean Jamaican with dreadlocks framing his friendly face. Wearing a white cotton shirt, back linen jacket and faded jeans, threadbare at the knees, his sandaled feet seem always in motion to the sound of an inner tune.

The educational value of MUDs is not so much in maneuvering around in these text-based virtual environments, but in creating them -- and you create them by describing them. Young people love these systems, and when they are asked to create their own place, they are motivated to build environments that are as realistic as possible, understanding that its realism is based on the richness of its description.

Below is a MUD session where Wiz logs in, meets Pei, and then starts to construct a giant Pyramid.

What Appears on the Screen[*]	Comments
WELCOME TO KIDSMUSH This Multi-User Domain is a sandbox for kids, a place where learners can build a place by describing, dream by doing, and learn by constructing. Please address questions to: david@landmark-project.com ---------------------------------- Use create <name> <password> to create a character. Use connect <name> <password> to connect to your existing character. Use QUIT to logout. Use the WHO command to find out who is online	This text appears when Wiz connects to the MUD using his MUD client software.

[*] Italicized characters represents text that was typed in by Wiz.

What Appears on the Screen[*]	Comments
currently.	
connect wiz opensesame	Wiz logs in by typing the word *connect* his login name and password.

Last connect was from 209.86.160.101 on Tue Jul 28 03:54:10 1998.Last connect was from 209.86.160.101 on Tue Jul 28 03:54:10 1998.
 	
MAIL: You have no mail.
 	
Oasis(#9RLnAJ)
 	
You are in the Omnar oasis. To the north, you see a spring fed pool of the bluest water. All around are palm trees, bending low under the relentless winds, but providing comforting shade for weary travelers, providing comforting shade for weary travelers.
 	
Obvious exits:
 	
  An inviting pool
  Sultan's tent
  caravan
	Upon admission, Wiz finds himself at the same place he stood the last time he logged out of the system.

sultan's tent	Wiz types in *sultan's tent*, one of the exits from the Oasis.
You bend over and slip under the flap, moving from the rumbling wind of the outside to the peace and quiet of the sultan's chambers. Sultan's Tent(#70RLnA) You see an enormous room, walled by tapestries. Several areas are arranged for conversation with pillows circled around low standing brass tables. Obvious exits:	Then he reads this result of his command.

What Appears on the Screen[*]	**Comments**
| ```
Out to the oasis
Room of Magic
``` | |
| ```
GAME: Pei has connected.

"Hello Pei!

You say, "Hello Pei!"
``` | After returning *back to the Oasis*, Pei shows up. Wiz types *"Hello Pei!* and you read *You say, "Hello Pei!"* Anyone else in the room, including Pei reads *Wiz says "Hello Pei!"* |
| ```
Pei says, "Hi Wiz! How are you
this evening?"

:turns two backward flips

Wiz turns two backward flips
``` | Pei returns the hello and then Wiz types *:turns to backward flips*. Everyone in this place reads *Wiz turns two backward flips*. |
| ```
look pei

Pei(#88PWenrAc?%)

You see a rather tall Jamaican
with dreadlocks. He wears a clean
white cotton shirt with a dark
linen jacket and faded jeans worn
to threads at the knees. His
sandaled feet seem always in
motion to some inner tune.
Carrying:

Walking Stick(#82n)
``` | Wiz types *look pei* and then reads the description of Pei'o'Pah. |
| ```
dig(Pyramid Entrance,Towering
Pyramid;Pyramid;tp;p,Out to the
Oasis;out;o)

Pyramid created with room number
74.
Opened.

Trying to link...

Linked.

Opened.
``` | Here, Wiz creates a Pyramid. The command is divided into four parts: **Dig** -- is the command to build a room. **Pyramid Entrance** -- is the name of the room. **Towering Pyramid;Pyramid; tp;p** -- The first item before the first semicolon is the entrance that people will see from outside the room. The following items are shorter |
```

What Appears on the Screen*	Comments
| ```
Trying to link...

Linked.
``` | alternatives that can be typed to enter the room.<br>**Out to the Oasis;out;o** -- The first item is the way out that people see from inside the room. The additional items are abbreviations. |
| ```
look

Oasis(#9RlnAJ)

You are in the Omnar oasis. To the
north, you see a spring fed pool
of the bluest water. All around
are palm trees, bending low under
the relentless winds, but
providing comforting shade for
weary travelers.
Contents:
Pei(#88PWenrAc?%)

Obvious exits:
  Towering Pyramid
  An inviting pool
  Sultan's tent
  caravan

Towering Pyramid

Pyramid(#74Rn)

Obvious exits:
  Out to the Oasis
``` | Wiz types *look* again to see the Oasis, but find that there is a new exit, Towering Pyramid.<br>Then he types *Towering Pyramid* to go into the new Pyramid. |
| ```
@describe #74=You find yourself in
a dark tunnel that seems to go on
forever, down into the base of the
structure.  To your right you can
barely make out hieroglyphs that
translate into a warning.

Pyramid - Set.
``` | The *@describe* command adds reality to the inside of the pyramid's entrance. In this command, Wiz use the object number in the place of the name.<br>After the description has been set. Wiz types *look* to see the room. |
```

What Appears on the Screen*	Comments

`look`
 	
`Pyramid(#74Rn)Pyramid(#74Rn)`
 	
`You find yourself in a dark tunnel`
`that seems to go on forever, down`
`into the base of the structure. To`
`your right you can barely make out`
`hieroglyphs that translate into a`
`warning.`
 	
`Obvious exits:`
`  Out to the Oasis`
	Additional rooms can be added to the same way that the Pyramid entrance was created. Students can continue to embellish their creations by editing and polishing their descriptions.

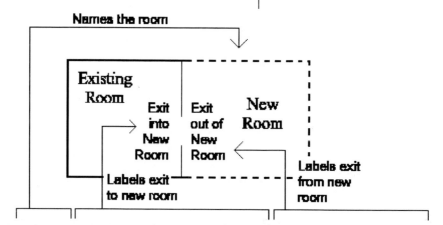

Dig(Pyramid,Towering Pyramid;pyramide;p,Out to the Oasis;oasis;o)

In 1992, I met Dr. Billie Hughes (Phoenix College, Phoenix, Arizona) through an Internet mailing list. I was becoming interested in MUDs at that time, and Billie invited me to their Camp Marimuse, a summer experience for elementary school aged students whom had been identified as "at risk" of failure. What they were doing at Marimuse was absolutely compelling. These children, who teachers couldn't get to write their names in the classroom, were writing megabytes of information in the process of creating their own virtual environment.

After the first camp was over, I invited Billie, and the teachers and volunteers who helped the students, to my virtual office at MIT (this was a text-based office that I had built on a MOO (Multi-user domain Object Oriented) at the Media Lab at MIT. The following is an excerpt of the interview that I conducted in my virtual studio, each of us literally sitting in our offices, homes, or classrooms.

Pei says, "Tell me about the students who participated in Camp MariMUSE?"

Woody says, "Do you want a feel for what they were like in RL, when they entered the room?"

Pei says, "Yes!"

Avalon sits back listening to those who were with the children the most to talk.

Miss-K says, "Well, it was quite a mixed group of children. Our school is very multi-ethnic and those groups were represented at the camp."

Avalon looks at Miss-K remembering just how diverse the group really was.

Miss-K says, "The kids were all going into the fourth, fifth or sixth grade."

Miss-K says, "The children who attended were children who were definitely at-risk for failure in school either because of their backgrounds or skills. They were chosen by the teachers at Longview on the basis of who we thought might benefit the most."

Platoon materializes out of thin air.

Platoon says, "HI Pei, sorry I interrupted"

Pei says, "Platoon, my man! gime five!"

Platoon ^5's Pei

Platoon sits back and listens

Woody says, "The first couple of days the children were very quiet and shy. After the comfort level was attained the kids were conversing in the muse and RL with real excitement and interest"

Miss-K nods.

Pei says, "How did the students first approach the text-based virtual environment?   What was their early reaction?"

Miss-K says, "On the first day, I heard whispers of, "This is dumb." By the end of the first session, all the campers agreed it was about the coolest thing they had ever done."

Pei says, "How did the parents react to Camp MariMUSE?"

Lila says, "Many parents had to take off work, with no pay, to attend any function to which they were invited. Such as graduation"

Wlad says, "Some even rode over on the school bus to be here."

Woody says, "When the parents first met with us, PC volunteers and Wlad, there was a very small turn out. After the camp was over there was almost 100 percent parent participation."

Lila says, "Running Wind's parents went to great lengths to attend graduation. They were VERY proud of him and his accomplishments."

Wlad says, "And parents who had never heard their children talk about what they were doing at school were getting rave reviews and daily updates on the camp activities."

Avalon says, "We had the superintendent who was amazed at the children's creativity and the amount of writing they did. We also had state representatives who felt the excitement. And we had parents who knew their kids were really excited about learning."

Avalon says, "Remember, this was only a 3 week camp. All of this happened in 3 short weeks."

Lila shakes her head, and says, "Hard to believe we did all that in 3 weeks."

Pei 's heart is full!

Pei says, "Were there any real surprises?"

Miss-K says, "It seemed like a magical time."

Lady Starlight nods.

Lila says, "I was very impressed with the increase in global awareness."

Miss-K says, "I was blown away by the research that the students initiated!"

Miss-K says, "It was a time of being completely accepted."

Avalon grins at Miss-K.

Avalon says, "They felt accepted for who they were, with no strings attached."

Lila nods in agreement

Miss-K says, "Actually, I still get misty eyed about it."

Avalon hands an embroidered hankie to Miss-K.

Miss-K giggles

Papers on Educational Applications of MUDs

Children, MUDs, and Learning	Billie Hughes & Jim Walters
http://pcacad.pc.maricopa.edu/Pueblo/writings/bib/AERA-paper-1995.html	
Building Intentional Networked Learning Communities	Billie Hughes & Jim Walters
http://pcacad.pc.maricopa.edu/td/aaaPaper.html	
Educational MUDs: Issues and Challenges	Billie Hughes
http://pcacad.pc.maricopa.edu/Pueblo/writings/bib/Issues//Billie-issues.html	
Use of MUDs to Improve Literacy	Cynde Welbes
http://pcacad.pc.maricopa.edu/Pueblo/writings/bib/Issues//welbes-issue.html	
Stories from Longview Teachers	Compiled by Billie Hughes
http://pcacad.pc.maricopa.edu/Pueblo/pueblo/Longview/	
Moose Crossing Proposal	Amy Bruckman
http://lucien.berkeley.edu/MOO/moose-crossing-proposal.ps	

MUD Client Software	
Vista (Windows 95)	http://pcacad.pc.maricopa.edu/Pueblo/clients/vista.html
MacMoose (Mac OS)	http://asb.www.media.mit.edu/people/asb/MacMOOSE
MUSH Client (Windows 95)	http://www.gammon.com.au/mushclient/mushclient.htm
ZMUD (Windows 3.x)	http://www.zuggsoft.com
MUDDweller	http://tucows.fastdata.net/mac/adnload/dlmuddwellmac.html

Education Related MUDs	
MediaMOO	http://www.cc.gatech.edu/fac/Amy.Bruckman/MediaMOO/
Moose Crossing	http://www.cc.gatech.edu/fac/Amy.Bruckman/moose-crossing/
Internet Public library MOO	http://www.ipl.org/moo/
Pueblo	http://pcacad.pc.maricopa.edu/Pueblo/index_frame.html

MUD Server Software	
PennMUSH Server for Win32	http://www.gammon.com.au/pennmush /win32mush.htm
PennMUSH Server for Mac OS	http://mac.pennmush.org

Rich Information Resources

For years, teachers have collected information from a wide variety of sources to use in their classrooms; information that supplements their textbooks. About twenty years ago, when my grandfather and grandmother were moving out of their large house, they gave me fifteen years worth of National Geographics. I received this gift because I was the only person in the family who was a schoolteacher. I am ashamed to say that when I got those historic magazines home and started leafing through the pages, I had scissors in my hands. I cut those precious magazines to pieces so that I could show my students pictures of the places and people I was teaching them about. These pictures, converted into learning center activities, gave my students brand new glimpses into cultures and environments that they had only heard or read about.

Today, the Internet provides teachers with a virtual warehouse of materials. You can find text, pictures, sound files, animations, and video clips, and you find them in abundance. This, however, is part of the problem -- finding them! When the World Wide Web is doubling in size every 90 days, finding the best information becomes a daunting challenge. The following sections describe strategies that will make you and your students more proficient Internet researchers.

Advanced Strategies for Searching the Internet

Mining the Internet is a metaphor frequently used to describe the act of searching the Internet. It works fairly well, especially within the context of one of this book's major themes, that information from the Internet should be viewed as a raw material, to be processed into new information products. However, when discussing the process of searching the Internet, the mining metaphor has one limitation. When mining the earth for iron or other mineral, there are also many miners, but only one or a small number of engineers. This engineer knows the earth and the clues that it exhibits, and then tells the miners where to dig.

In the same way that the detective at the scene of a crime gets an immediate impression of the events that transpired and then sets out to find clues and evidence that support that initial impression, Internet researchers use their assumptions about what is available and what they will find as clues for their search.

When searching the Internet, we are all miners and engineers. Each of us must know the technique for digging, but also be skilled in seeking out clues so that we can create strategies for knowing where to dig. Perhaps the most important thing to understand about searching for information on the Internet is the fact that it is more like being a detective than being a miner.

When researchers approach the Internet, they are looking for information on a certain topic. Usually, they already have an idea of what they will find...

- The type of Internet resource that will hold the information -- college course, commercial, or educational web site, or perhaps a mailing list archive,
- Other information that might be included on the same web page, and
- Whether the information is likely to be of a general or specialized nature.

In the same way that the detective at the scene of a crime gets an immediate impression of the events that transpired and then sets out to find clues and evidence that support that initial impression, Internet researchers use their assumptions about what is available and what they will find as clues for their search. As a crime detective keeps an eye open for evidence that paints a different story, successful Internet researchers are open to different types of information that they had not anticipated, resources and formats that were not expected.

Because searching the Internet means investigating a digital information world, it is important to understand that researching on the Internet is a process. It is almost never a single search with your favorite search engine identifying the best solution for your problem at the top of a list of 30,000 hits. Success comes from a series of searches, each revealing new clues, new avenues, and ultimately, the best information for your needs.

Today's search tools make the Internet appear, at least, to be organized.

Earlier tools for finding resources on the Internet included programs like *Archie*, *Veronica*, and *Jughead* -- names owing to the eccentricities of the programmers who developed the tools. A popular analogy during those years was that the Internet was a lot like a used bookstore ---------- after an earthquake. Today's tools make the Internet appear, at least, to be organized. They enable more systematic approaches to Internet research and more success, which is especially impressive considering the geometric growth of the global electronic library.

There are essentially three tools or categories of tools that you can use to find digital resources on the Internet. The following sections will discuss each.

1. Topic Oriented Directories

Using topic-oriented directories is very much like browsing a library. You look for the shelves that hold books about the topic you are looking for, and then you walk along those shelves looking for the right book or books.

Topic-oriented directories organize Internet resources logically, by subject. They organize the resources in a hierarchical structure providing a list of general subjects, each subject leading to a list of topics within that subject, each topic leading to subtopics, and usually to more subtopics. Eventually, you are presented with a list of Internet resources or web sites, each related to the final subtopic that you selected.

A Sample Search

When asked about search tools, the one that most people think of first is Yahoo. This valuable and popular search service has been around for many years. Let's use Yahoo to search for web pages about Monarch Butterflies. We will begin by going to the Yahoo front page at:

http://www.yahoo.com

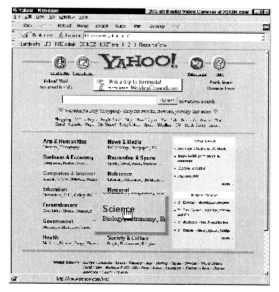

During this hunt, we scan the list of major subjects and select **Science** as the one that will most likely lead to information about monarch butterflies.

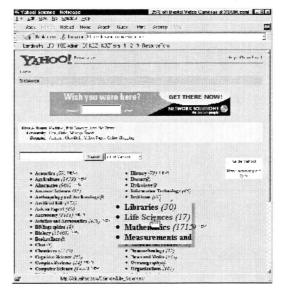

We scan through a fairly long list of topics related to science. From the list we select **Life Science**.

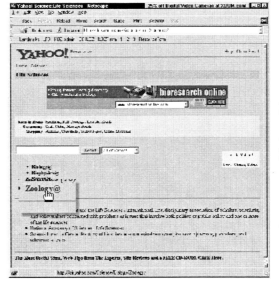

As we scan through the **Life Science** topics, **Zoology** makes the most sense for including information about butterflies.

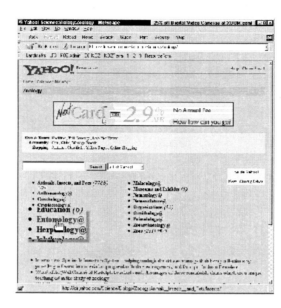

Entomology, the study of insects is our choice from the **Life Science** page.

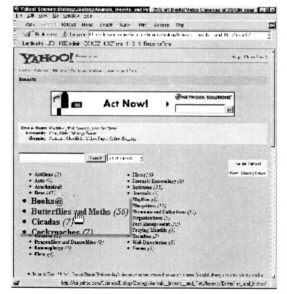

After clicking **Butterflies and Moths**, we are presented with a small list of web sites, all of them about butterflies and moths.

Advantages of Searching with Topic Oriented Directories

1. Topic oriented directories rely on a logical organization of information. Unlike encyclopedias and other reference books that organize information in alphabetical order, topic directories are organized by subject and topic. Therefore, the information (rather than spelling) becomes the navigator. Another benefit of this information-based organization is that different research topics can be logically linked together in a variety of ways, resulting in valuable cross-references.

2. The second advantage lies in the final page that we received. That final list of web pages will be a short and concentrated list of resources, concentrated in that all of the sites will be about butterflies and moths. If you have used a larger search engine before, such as Alta Vista or Hotbot, you know that a search of butterflies will produce a very large list of resources, only some of which are actually about butterflies. For instance a search of **Altavista** generated a list of 264,150 web pages with the word *butterflies* or *butterfly* in them. By contrast, **Yahoo** produced a list of only 37 sites, each one of which is about butterflies.

Disadvantages of Searching with Topic Oriented Directories

1. Search engine indexes are built by software. It is an automated process. Topic oriented directories, on the other hand, are built and organized by people who examine each registered web site in order to place it in its most logical place in the topic tree. Therefore, search engines tend to grow much larger much more quickly. A result is that when you get a list of web sites by browsing a topic directory, you are only getting a small fraction of the resources that you would get from a search engine, only a minute fraction of what is available on the Internet.

    Now that fraction of resources will most likely be of higher quality, on the average, than much of what you would get through a search engine. People are selecting the sites that go into the topic directories, while search engines add almost anything to their indexes. Yet, much will be missed by relying only on topic directories.

2. Another disadvantage of using topic directories is the fact that they are time consuming. Moving through the subject paths can lead to dead ends and result in many false starts and backtrackings. But a very important thing to understand about searching the Internet is that it does take time. Remember that you are an information detective, investigating a digital universe.

Some Topic Oriented Directories

Topic Oriented Directories	
Service	**URL**
Yahoo	http://www.yahoo.com
Yahooligans Yahoo for children	http://www.yahooligans.com
Galaxy	http://galaxy.einet.net
NewHoo	http://www.newhoo.com
Netscape Netcenter	http://home.netscape.com
Internet Start	http://home.microsoft.com
LookSmart	http://www.snap.com
Snap	http://www.looksmart.com
Apali Spanish Languages Directory	http://www.apali.com/
Native Search Directory of Native American web resources	http://nativesearch.com
Education Related Directories	
G.R.A.D.E.S. -- Classroom Connect	http://www.classroom.net/Grades
Kathy Schrock's Guide for Educators	http://www.capecod.net/schrockguide/
Planet K-12	http://planetk-12.planetsearch.com/
Blue Web'n	http://www.kn.pacbell.com/wired/bluewebn/categories.html
Link-o-Rama -- Global School House	http://www.gsn.org/links/
Rusk High School Library's Web Guide	http://www.tyler.net/ruskhslib/default.htm

2. Search Engines

Search engines are the miracle of the Internet. These sophisticated tools seem to reach right into the global network and scour its contents at your command. In reality, they do not work exactly in this way, although the true nature of search engines is no less fascinating. Technically, in order to be called a *Search Engine*, a search tool must be made up of three major components:

1. **The Interface**

2. **An Index**

3. **Crawlers or Spiders**

The Interface

This is the search engine's web page. More specifically, the interface is the way that we talk to the search engine: the buttons we click, the menus we pull down, and the text boxes we fill. A great deal of research and study goes into the design of search engine pages, and their design is constantly evolving in order to make their operation easier for people and more effective.

The Index

The index is a database that operates behind the web page. It holds information about thousands, or millions, or

Some Internet Lore

Lycos (www.lycos.com) was the first true search engine. Until that time, search tools such as Yahoo relied on people to add resource descriptions and URLs. Lycos, on the other hand, sent spiders out looking for new Internet resources. *Lycos Arachnid* is Latin for *wolf spider*. The wolf spider is the only spider that leaves its den to hunt for prey rather than trapping it in a web. In much the same way, the Lycos search engine sends its spiders out hunting for new web pages as opposed to the older Yahoo waiting for people to drop web pages into its web.

hundreds of millions of web pages. When your search engine is searching, it is actually searching this database. Different search engine's databases represent varying amounts of the Internet. No search engine can represent the entire Internet. Some search engines have large indexes and other have small ones. Sometimes your searches will be more effective when you use smaller index search engines and some times you are better using large ones. It depends on what you are looking for and why.

Crawlers or Spiders

This is what really makes a search engine unique. Crawlers or spiders are computer programs that, in a sense, are crawling through the Internet, like spiders crawling across a web. They do this by continually searching through web pages, looking for hyperlinks that were not present the last time they came through. When they find a new link, they follow it, many times discovering a brand new web page. Then the spiders collect the information they need from the new page and return to the search engine to add the new data to engine's index. Search Engines grow automatically as a result of these crawlers or spiders.

The Language of Search Engines

Search engines are your helpers. They are information assistants who aid you in finding the information that you need to solve a problem, answer a question, or make a decision. Like any other assistant, the degree to which they are able to help depends on the degree to which you are able to tell them what you want. Therefore, communicating with your search engine is a critical part of the search process.

Search engines need to know what information you seek, and they need this information communicated in a logical way -- they are, after all, computers. The language that we traditionally use to talk with computer-based searching tools is called *Boolean*, named after George Boole, a mathematician of the 19th century.

In *Boolean Logic* we use **keywords** to describe what words to look for when searching the index. We also use **operators** to describe the relationships between our **keywords** and the information that we need. The most frequently used **operators** are **AND**, **OR**, and **NOT**.

Let's use an example to explore how we would use *Boolean Logic* to search for information on the Internet. We will look for information about Native Americans in the state of Ohio. In the table below we will explore several concepts involved in speaking Boolean and relate these concepts to our search.

Concept	Explanation/Example
Keyword	A keyword is a word or term that we believe will be present (or should not be present) in the web pages that we seek. These are the words that we want our search engine to look for. In our example, one word that would likely appear in a web page about Native Americans is *Indian*.
	Example: Indian
OR	In many cases, there may be a synonym of our keyword that might appear in the web page instead of the keyword we have already chosen. To make certain that we do not miss any of these pages, we add the synonym and then separate the two words with the **operator**, **OR**. In the case of our example, many web pages would likely use the term *Native American*, which is commonly used today in the place of *Indian*. In this case we would use the operator, **OR**, to say that we want web pages with either the word *Indian* or the term *Native American*.
	Example: Indian OR Native American
AND	Since we are looking for information about Native Americans in the state of Ohio, then an additional keyword that will be present in the web pages that we seek is *Ohio*. We want to narrow the web pages that we get to only those about Native Americans in Ohio, so we will say that both terms must be present. Here is where we will use AND.
	Example: Indian OR Native American AND Ohio

NOT	As we think through the information that we are likely to receive, we realize that there is a baseball team in Cleveland, Ohio called the Indians. We will want to filter out all web pages about the baseball team. So we will add a new keyword, *baseball*, and connect it to our search express with the operator, **Not**. We are saying that desired web pages should NOT have the keyword *baseball* in them.
	Example: Indian OR Native American AND Ohio NOT baseball

quotes	Just as we use commas, question marks, and other punctuation to help communicate with people, we use special symbols to clarify what we want from a search engine. One example is the use of quotation marks to define phrases. In our example, Native American is going to look like two separate words to the search engine that could each appear any place in the web page. To communicate that these two words belong together as a distinct phrase, we use quotes.
	Example: Indian OR "Native American" AND Ohio NOT baseball

Parentheses

Each **operator** in a search expression defines a distinct *keyword concept.*

> *keyword 1* AND k*eyword 2*

> *keyword 3* OR *keyword 4*

> *keyword 5* NOT k*eyword 6*

A keyword concept can consist of:

A single keyword

> [*keyword 1*]

Two single keywords or phrases connected by an operator

> [*keyword 1* OR *keyword 2*] AND [*keyword 3*]

Keyword concepts connected by an operator to other keyword concepts.

> [*keyword 1* OR *keyword 2* AND *keyword 3*] AND [*keyword 4* OR *keyword 5*]

Individual keyword concepts are usually marked by enclosing them in parentheses. In our example, the following are distinct keyword concepts:

> (Indian OR "Native American")

> ((Indian OR "Native American") AND Ohio)

The final keyword concept, the one that includes all constituent keyword concepts is called our search expression.

Another way of thinking about search concepts and expressions is mathematically. George Boole was, after all, a mathematician. If you think in terms of *order of operations*, this is exactly what the parentheses do in our search expression. It defines what keywords to search, and what relationships to test first. You may find your best example in algebra, where these two examples illustrate the same concept in Boolean searching and algebra.

Boolean -- ((Indian OR "Native American") AND Ohio)

Algebra -- ((A + B) X C)

Example: ((Indian OR "Native American") AND Ohio) NOT baseball

It is important to note at this point that Boolean Logic is much easier to understand than it is to teach. Yet those who understand know that it is a very effective way of communicating to your search engine your information needs.

To make things easier for casual users, Internet search engines have developed alternatives to traditional Boolean Logic. One of the most common conventions is the use of pluses (+) and minuses (-), to indicate which terms must (+) and must not (-) be present in the web pages listed by your search engine.

An Alternative Search Convention

Pluses (+)	Any keywords in your search expression that MUST appear in your target web page should be preceded by a plus symbol (+). If the keyword is a phrase, then it should be enclosed by quotes
	Example: +basketball +"Mike Jordan"
Minuses (-)	Any keyword that must NOT appear in your target web page should be preceded by a minus symbol (-). As when using the plus symbol, if the keyword is a phrase, then it should be enclosed by quotes.
	Example: +basketball +"Mike Jordan" -Nike

Pipe (|) This character is usually above the backslash (\\) on your keyboard	The pipe character helps you to fine-tune your search. Placing a pipe character between two search terms tells the search engine to search for the first term and then search for the second term within the first term's hits. Example: Internet|Web

Advantages of Using Search Engines

1. The indexes of search engines are usually vast, representing significant portions of the Internet and offering links to a wide variety and quantity of information resources.

2. The growing sophistication of search engine software enables us to precisely describe the information that we seek.

3. The large number and variety of search engines enriches the Internet, making it at least appear to be organized.

Disadvantages of Using Search Engines

1. Regardless of the growing sophistication, many well thought-out search phrases produce list after list of irrelevant web pages. The typical search still requires sifting through dirt to find the gems.

2. Using search engines does involve a learning curve. Many beginning Internet users, because of the disadvantage above, become discouraged and frustrated.

Some Internet Search Engines

Search Engine	URL
Alta Vista	http://www.altavista.digital.com
Excite	http://www.excite.com
HotBot	http://www.hotbot.com
Infoseek	http://www.infoseek.com

Lycos	http://www.lycos.com

Kid Friendly Search Engines *(Crawler style search engines that work to filter out adult material)*

Ask Jeeves	http://www.ajkids.com/
Disney Internet Guide (DIG)	http://www.disney.com/dig/today/
Lycos SafetyNet	http://personal.lycos.com/safetynet/safetynet.asp

Meta Search Engines *(search engines that search other search engines)*

MetaCrawler	http://www.metecrawler.com
DogPile	http://www.dogpile.com
Highway 61	http://www.highway61.com

3. Net-Smarts

OK, this is not a computer tool. It is not hardware or software, but net-smarts is perhaps your most valuable tool in finding information on the Internet. It is a growing awareness of what is available on the Internet and how it works, and a growing sense of "where is the best first place to start?" As mentioned earlier, searching the Internet involves investigating an information environment, turning over stones, checking for fingerprints, examining strands of hair. It means having an idea of what you are looking for, and at the same time being open for the unexpected.

More than anything, being net-smart involves asking questions.

More than anything, being net-smart involves asking questions. Here are some questions that must be asked and considered when embarking on an information safari on the Internet.

1. What do you want to find?

2. Will the information most likely be found in articles, commercial web pages, software archives, conference proceedings, discussion groups, or from people. The answer to this question helps you decide on a search strategy.

3. Why would someone publish this information on the Internet?

4. Who would publish this information on the Internet?

5. Who would host this a web page with this information on it?

6. What would a web page with the Information I seek look like?

    Questions two through five would each help us in developing our search phrase.

7. Are you wanting to broaden your knowledge of a general topic or do you want more narrow, specific information?

> **Broad or general information is usually best found in topic-oriented directories. More information on more specific topics is best found with search engines.**

The S.E.A.R.C.H. Process

Conducting effective searches of the Internet is rarely an issue of typing in a single keyword and being presented with the solution to your problem. It is much more frequently a series of searches, each revealing more clues about the information that is available, and where that information can be found.

Developing a search process can be difficult, because each person's process depends on their personal style of using information and the particular types of information that they typically need. However, there is a process that can be used as a springboard to the personal procedures that you develop with experience. The process is called S.E.A.R.C.H. It is an acronym for the process that has you **Start** with a small database search tool, **Edit** your search expression, **Advance** to a larger database search tool, **Refine** your search phrase, **Cycle** back and advance again, and finally, **Harvest** your information gems.

On the next page is a larger representation of the S.E.A.R.C.H. process.

Search Strategy

Search with a key term on Yahoo or another small index search tool.

You start with a small index search tool for two reasons:

1. You will receive a limited and manageable number of hits.
2. The hits that you get will be representative of what is available on the subject

Examine the hit pages collecting words that are common among the relevant hits and words that are common among the irrelevant hits.

Edit the search expression with terms gleaned from the initial search.

Add words collected from the initial search, including words common among relevant and irrelevant pages. Construct a Boolean search expression that effectively communicates the information that you seek.

Advance to a larger index search engine

Enter the edited search phrase into a larger index search tool. Examples are:
- Excite   http://www.excite.com
- InfoSeek   http://www.infoseek.com
- Alta Vista   http://www.altavista.digital.com
- HotBot   http://www.hotbot.com

Refine the search expression

Explore the pages reported by the larger search engine and refine the expression even more, further defining the relevant hits, and filtering the irrelevant. Again, examine both good hits and bad hits.

Cycle back and Advance again.

Return to the advanced search engine that you used before or use another search engine.

Harvest the results

Collect the needed information by printing, downloading, forwarding by e-mail or just reading.

Finding and Accessing Instructional Materials

Being about to put on your detective's hat and investigate the digital frontier for information is an essential skill, especially for educators. However, it is equally important to grow a list of web sites that you find to be consistently rich and appropriate for your needs. Here is a list of sites that are in my bookmarks. You can start here and grow your own list.

Service & URL	Description
Landmarks for Schools	This web site is dedicated to providing teachers with links to information raw materials with which they can create learning resources and their students can construct information products. http://www.landmark-project.com/
PBS Online	This web site offers a wide variety of resources for teachers to be used in conjunction with PBS programming. http://www.pbs.org/
Discovery Channel Online	Like PBS, this web site offers materials and other opportunities to be used with their programming. http://www.discovery.com/
The History Channel	This site has a wealth of material. One of the most interesting resources is *Great Speeches*, an archive of recordings (Real Audio files) of great speeches of our century. The include Mahatma Ghandi, Jimmy Hoffa, George Bernard Shaw, and Babe Ruth. http://www.historychannel.com
CNN Interactive	This rich web site hold a large number of resources for teachers of just about any discipline. One valuable resource is the *Transcripts* service which stores the text transcripts for CNN programming over the past week or so. http://cnn.com/TRANSCRIPTS/

CNN Interactive Video Archive	*Video Archive* is another useful service. It is a searchable database of video files (QuickTime). A search of *biotechnology* returned 76 clips. http://cnn.com/video_vault/
CNN Interactive Custom News	CNN offers another service that could be useful for teachers. Called *Custom News*, teachers can indicate the specific issues that they are interested in based on current and upcoming units of study, and CNN will build a custom page with links to current stories on those issues. http://cnn.com/CustomNews/
Earth Science Enterprise from NASA	This rich resources provides links to a wide variety of web sites falling under each of the following categories: air, water, land, life, sun. http://www.hq.nasa.gov/office/ese/science/ Earth Science Enterprise also has an archive of images that can be used in learning materials. http://www.hq.nasa.gov/office/ese/gallery/

Processing Information Found on the Internet

Evaluating Internet Resources

There was a time, only a few years ago, when all you had to say was, "I got this information from the Internet," and it was considered gospel. At that time, the only people who could publish on this growing network were research centers and Universities, and the information was almost exclusively scholarly in nature.

Today, just about anyone can publish on the Internet. People can bypass the editors and selection committees and make their information almost instantly available to a global audience -- and it costs almost nothing.

This presents many problems for those of us who use digital information. But it is important to note that these problems are neither unique nor brand new. Critical evaluation of information has been necessary since humankind first learned to communicate and it has been part of what we have taught in classrooms for years. Yet never before has it become so easy for so many to communicate so effectively and so broadly. This makes critical evaluation of information more important than ever before -- perhaps even a "basic skill." How do you tell if it's the truth and valuable?

The Problems

There are three major considerations in evaluating Internet resources:

1. Reliability

2. Credibility

3. Perspective & Purpose

Reliability

The reliability of information from the Internet refers most often to the correctness of the information. However, the issue is complicated by time factors and other constraints that can render information undependable. In this day of rapid change and in a world where our audiences cross cultural boundaries with increasing frequency, it becomes more difficult to rely on information. We must go beyond asking if the information is accurate, and explore under what conditions it will remain accurate. What is true today may not be true tomorrow. What is true for this culture many not be true for that. Will the information remain reliable and relevant for the duration of the information product you or your students are producing and will it be relevant for all of the cultures represented by your audience?

Credibility

Credibility refers more to the origins of the information. Does the author and/or the publishing organization have the authority to produce the information and to present it the way that they have? There should be information about the author or links to a web page that present his or her credentials. Along with these credentials should be links to other documents that the author has published. If this information is not present, then your research is not over. You must research the author over the Internet to learn what else he or she has written or what others have written about the author.

Perspective & Purpose

Perspective & Purpose refers to bias. What does the author or publishing organization have to gain by publishing this information? Is there a reason why they would want to present it in a particular way or from a certain angle? Are they selling a product? Are they supporting a specific political agenda? Do they have an axe to grind?

There are several questions to ask about the information you have found:

Collecting Information about Authors & Publishing Organizations

Let's say that we are using the Internet to find information about evaluating Internet-based information, and we find an article written by **David Warlick** and published by the **Media Awareness Network** of Canada.

http://www.media-awareness.ca/eng/med/class/teamed2/warlick.htm

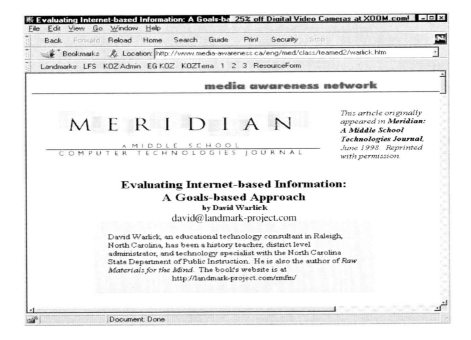

The only thing that we have right away is the name of the author and his e-mail address, the name of the organization, and the URL of the article. Following are some techniques that we can use to learn more about the author and the publishing organization.

Evaluative Investigation Techniques

E-mail the Author

We can send an e-mail message to the author asking him where he got the ideas for his article. Ask about any research that he conducted or examined or any related information that is available on the Internet or in print. When someone publishes information, he or she should be willing to support it.

Research the Author

Simply use the Internet to research the author or publishing organization. Using a search engine to research the author not only reveals other writings and services by the author, but also what other people are saying about his work.

Who's Backing the Author?

Since the domain of the author's e-mail address is unique (not @aol.com or @hotmail.com, we might try accessing a web page with the domain. We would try to access: http://www.landmark-project.com? If we find that the organization that is providing Mr. Warlick with an e-mail address sells a product that he is promoting, then we have an indication of possible bias. We can continue to investigate the site if appropriate, looking for mission statements, products (not just for sale) that related to the article, and references to the author.

Who's Standing Behind the Curtain?

We can also check the owner of the Landmarks for Schools web site by learning who owns the URL. Who owns the domain, www.landmark-project.com. We can go to the web site of the company who manages domains, **Network Solutions**, and access their database of domain names. We go to:

http://www.internic.com

Here we type the domain, *landmark-project.com* into the form and click the Search button. After a moment we receive a report on who owns and maintains the domain name for the web server.

Backtracking the URL

We can find more information about the publishing organization by examining the article's URL. Backtracking a URL involves removing its elements one by one. Each element is separated by a forward slash (/). So we start removing element to the right until we get another web page:

http://www.media-awareness.ca/eng/med/class/teamed2/warlick.htm

> After we have removed the first two elements
> (teamed2/warlick.htm), and then press the **Enter** key, we see a
> web page that appears to be a resource page for teachers. We
> backup again until we receive another web page.

http://www.media-awareness.ca/eng/med/class/teamen2/warlick.htm

> Here we get the English version of the **Media Awareness
> Network** home page. We can explore this page and connected
> pages for information that would be helpful in determining any
> bias in their choosing to publish Mr. Warlick's work.

Goals-Based Evaluation of Internet Resources

There are a number of questions to be asked when evaluating
information from the Internet:

- Is the information accurate?
- Under what conditions will it remain accurate?
- Does the author have the authority or the credentials to
  produce this information?
- What does the author or publishing organization have to
  gain by publishing this information or by presenting it in
  this specific way?

However, there is another essential question to ask.

- Why do you need the information? What do you want to
  accomplish with this information, or with the information
  product you are creating?

The following is an edited version of an article that was first published in the North Carolina State University online journal, **Meridian** (http://www.ncsu.edu/meridian/). The title of the article is *Evaluating Internet-based Information: A Goals-based Approach.*[*]

The Scenario

A high school junior decides to write a report about the Holocaust for extra credit. It is a topic that her class has not yet discussed. At home our student uses her computer and access to the Internet to research the topic and word processing software to construct her report. She spends an hour searching the Internet and examining a variety of web sites about the subject. She selects three sites that are especially compelling because of the quality of the graphics and layout of the pages -- indicating to her, authority.

Our young woman copies text from the pages, carefully paraphrases some, quotes others, downloads images and pastes them into the appropriate spots on her file, prints a professional looking report with a color inkjet printer, and proudly turns it into the teacher two days later. She has used the Internet to explore and discover, and information processing technology to craft and report information about this historic event.

As can easily happen today, each of the web sites that our student used were published by neo-nazi and white-supremacist organizations portraying a biased point of view -- and our youngster's report becomes a reflection of this divisive perspective without the student even knowing it.

What is the Difference?

This kind of scenario has many educators concerned about using the Internet as a reliable resource for academic information. However, the presence of inaccurate and biased information on the Internet is not our only problem, and it may not even be the primary problem. Although our information system is expanding beyond the controlled environment to the uncontrollable Internet,

---

[*] Warlick, David F. "Evaluating Internet-based Information: A Goals-based Approach" Meridian Online Journal, North Carolina State University. 1998. http://www.ncsu.edu/meridian/jun98/feat2-6/feat2-6.html (April 1999).

the information and points of view have not really changed. What has changed dramatically is our tools.

Today, our students use professional and sophisticated information tools and global electronic networks to complete their assignments while most of us, in our day, used pencil and paper and the information resources that existed in our school library. While we did our work with what could be compared to a $12 box of Lincoln Logs, students today have at their disposal professional tools and virtually limitless materials, as if they have an entire *Builder's Supply* warehouse to work from. While we assembled our reports with children's building blocks, today's students can craft their information products with word processors, enrich them with

multimedia mined from the Internet, and empower them with hypertext. Their work can be compelling and it can be published to a global community.

The real problem with the scenario above is the assignment. The problem is that we are still, all to often, giving Lincoln Log assignments -- "Write a report about the Holocaust." The advanced and powerful capabilities that are increasingly available to our students beg for different kinds of tasks. Writing a report **about** something has as its goal the demonstration of gained knowledge. Yet gaining knowledge becomes only a small part of what students should be learning to prepare them for a world where knowledge changes and information grows at dizzying speeds. In fact, in the information world, their jobs will be to help in growing knowledge by becoming information builders.

From the perspective of the builder, our students have aisles of information processing tools to choose from and an Internet warehouse from which to select building materials. The difference is that the builder, in the middle of Builder's Supply, has a task or project in mind, something that he or she plans to build for the enjoyment and convenience of others. Our builder has a goal behind his or her selection of tools, lumber, and nails.

Likewise, as students browse through the Internet looking for information raw materials, they too should have goals for their work. The difference between "Lincoln Log" assignments and what students should be doing today, is that our young high school junior should have had a goal for her report beyond that of just earning a grade. Because she can produce such impressive work and it can potentially be published for others to see and use, her goal should be behavioral. **Students should be building their information products to affect impressions, decisions, beliefs, support or defeat positions, or create new knowledge.**

Benefits of Goals-based projects

Goals-based projects provide an authentic context for the student's work. What they are learning and building is connected in some way with their experience and with the world around them. They are collecting, synthesizing, processing, assembling and expressing information for a reason that is real and beyond the mere pursuit of a grade.

When students are engaged in accomplishing a goal, beyond that of simply demonstrating knowledge, they are far less likely to complete their assignment by merely copying and pasting large chunks of text into their word processor. This is not to say that copying and pasting text from the Internet is wrong. This is what you do with digital information. When students are accomplishing goals:

- They collect and copy smaller chunks of information,

- Create mortar that holds the chunks together and lend them relevance to each other and to the expressed goal,

- Assemble the chunks and mortar,

- Producing unique and valuable information products.

Goals-based assignments also lend themselves especially well to the use of student produced rubrics. The student's goals can become part of the rubric's goals, with teacher or student defined benchmarks. This gives students a ruler with which to measure their success and teachers have a tool to assess the student's learning.

Goals-based Evaluation

What do goals-based assignments have to do with evaluating
Internet resources? Let's return to the builder's analogy. My father
was an avid wood worker. He built a wonderful woodworking
shop in our basement and spent many hours constructing furniture.
Sadly, it is a quality that he did not pass on to me. One of the
many things that my father taught me, though, is that when you are
building something, the number one key to success is using the
appropriate tools and materials. Walk into any "Builder's Supply,"
and you have a virtual Internet of tools and building materials
available to you. As you examine them individually, they are not
judged as good or bad, but simply appropriate or inappropriate for
specific building projects. Our task, as the shopper, is to select the
tools and materials that are appropriate to our goals.

Traditionally, Internet resources have been evaluated from the
perspective of the information itself and it's source. This usually
involves some type of checklist that puts all Internet information
through the same sieve, evaluating each based on the same criteria.

As students' information products should be based on teacher or
student established goals, evaluating the material that they consider
using in their products should also be goals-oriented. Rather than
judging the material based solely on itself via a standard
examination instrument, it should be judged from the perspective
of what the student wants to accomplish.

From this standpoint, we would not ask, "Is the author qualified?",
but, "What aspects of the author's background help me accomplish
my goal?" Under certain circumstances, a web page published by a
Neo-NAZI organization might actually be appropriate for an
assignment, while other resources, produced by people with
credentials would not. It depends on what the student wants to
accomplish.

This approach actually serves three interesting purposes:

1. The evaluation process seeks to draw in supporting or appropriate information rather than focusing on filtering "bad" information out.

2. The student gathers information about the information.

3. As students approach information with their goals to accomplish, they are less likely to be influenced by the goals of those who generated and published the information, which has interesting implications for *media literacy.*

Information about the Information

The second of the above benefits is of particular interest as Internet-based information meets with increasing suspicion. When creating an information product in the print-based world, it was usually enough to include a standard citation in the bibliography and to mention the author's name and a vague reference to the source to introduce the information. For instance, "John Robinson writes in his book, <u>Acres of Sound</u>, that...".

This would not be enough justification for information gathered from the wild Internet. It would not be enough to say, "John Robinson, in his web site http://... writes that..." Other rationale is necessary, and it might read like this:

John Robinson, in his twelve-month research at the University of Hawaii on the influences of motor sounds on the navigation of sea mammals, states in his web site (http://...) that...

This more elaborate explanation of the information's source lends it credibility when a mere URL would not. Therefore, part of the evaluation process should be to identify and collect this sort of supporting information about the information as justification. The form that is described in the next section will help in collecting information about the information.

A Goals-based Internet Evaluation Form

The form below has been created to help students evaluate Internet resources based on the goal(s) of their work. It begins with a statement of the student's goals, and then follows through with the collection of specific information with explanations of how the information supports the resource in terms of the student's goals.

Another assumption provides an additional basis for this form. As students are researching the Internet, we might safely assume that they are using a computer. Therefore, they should also be using a computer-based form for their evaluation and collection of information. This form is designed for this purpose. The student will come to the computer with a disk, and will complete the form(s) by typing their information into the appropriate spaces or by copying and pasting the information from the **Edit** menu.

The form on the next page is available on the Internet as a compressed file (.zip). The file will expand into three different versions of the form:

1.   Microsoft Word97 for Windows, (importable into Word97 for Win95 and Word98 for Mac OS)

2.   Rich Text Format (RTF-- importable into most any other word processing program)

3.   Text or ASCII file for computers with limited memory where only NotePad or SimpleText can be run along with the browser.

Internet Information Evaluation & Collection Form

Project Name:	
What is the goal of your project?	
Resource Name:	
Resource URL:	
Document Contact's Address:	
Author's Name:	
Publishing Organization:	
What aspect(s) of the author's or publishing organization's background helps you accomplish your goal?	
Date of Publishing:	
Date of Last revision:	
How does the date of the information's publishing or latest revision help you accomplish your goal?	
Information Format (text, columnar, picture, movie):	
How does the format of the information help you accomplish your goal?	
Paste information here:	
How does the content of the Information help you accomplish your goal?	
MLA-Style Citation Template:	

Author's Lastname, Author's Firstname. "Title of Document." Title of Complete Work (if applicable). Version or File Number, if applicable. Document date or date of last revision (if different from access date). Protocol and address, access path or directories (date of access).

The form on the previous page can be downloaded from the
Internet at the following URL. Note that there is a space between
"Desktop" & "Folder".

ftp://landmark-project.com/TLP/Desktop Folder/landmark/workshops/evaluation.zip

Description of the Form Sections

Project Name:
The project name labels the evaluated resource assigning it to a
specific project. Asking students to assign a project name can also
help them to think through their goals and to apply an identity to
the project based on those goals.

What is the goal of your project?
Here the students will enter the goal(s) of their project in words
that make it easy to associate other information resources to the
goal(s) at hand. Again, the goals should be behavioral. For
instance, how do you want to affect

- What the readers believe,

- Their impressions,

- How they makes decisions,

- Their knowledge, etc.

Resource Name:
This is the name of the web site, ftp file, picture, graph, or map
file.

Resource URL:
Enter the URL or electronic address of the Internet resource being
evaluated and retrieved so that it can be revisited at a later date.

Author's Name:
Find the name of the person who authored or compiled the
information. This is not always the webmaster of the page, and it
may be necessary from time to time to ask for the author's name
from the webmaster via e-mail. Another piece of information that
might be valuable here is the author's home page URL. In many

instances it is also good to have the name and e-mail address of the site's web master. He or she is usually the first contact point for the information being published.

Publishing Organization:
This is the organization that maintains the web or ftp site, or who sponsored the publishing of the information. In many cases the publishing organization and the author are the same. Again, the URL for the organization's home page might also be included in this space.

What aspect(s) of the author's or publishing organization's background helps you accomplish your goal?
This should include information about the author and the publishing organization that relates to the published information and that relates to the student's goals. This might also include special research in which the author is engaged or previous projects.

Another example might be the mission statement of the publishing organization. It could also involve the research that lead to the information and other studies being conducted by the author. Students should examine this information and pull out aspects that are relevant to the topic and that lend credence to the information and its relationship to the student's information product goals.

Date of Publishing:
Enter the date that the information was originally published. If it was published separately in print and this information is available on the web site, include this date as well.

Date of Last revision:
This information is not always available. In some cases information web resources are not updated, just published. This information will, however, be important for time sensitive data.

How does the date of the information's publishing or latest revision help you accomplish your goal?
In many cases the more recent the information is, the more valuable it is. However, this is not always the case. Sometimes, depending on the goals of the information product, information generated in 1942 or 1166 may lend it more valuable to the goal(s). In this section fill in any information about the publishing and

revision dates of the information that enhance the information product in relation to its goal(s).

Information Format (text, columnar, picture, movie):
Enter the format of the information here.

How does the format of the information help you accomplish your goal?
Information format is of greater importance than most people believe. In information rich environments, it is essential that information communicate itself as effectively as possible -- and this involves format. Some types of information deliver themselves into the understanding of readers by being displayed in columns and rows of text or numbers. Others communicate better as graphs and others as paragraphs of text.

Another consideration in this section is the transfer of Internet information from one format to another. The information may come as tabular data, but you need to convert it to graph to more effectively communicate the information. All of these notes should be entered in this section of the evaluation form.

Paste the information here.
One of the advantages of retrieving digital information from the Internet is the fact that it can conceivably be accessed, manipulated, included in the information product, and published without ever being printed to paper. Data can easily be copied from a web page or other Internet tool and then pasted into this section. If you are using MSWord or other more sophisticated word processor (especially if you are using a Macintosh), even pictures can be copied from the web and pasted into the evaluation.

How does the content of the Information help you accomplish your goal?
Why is this information important to accomplishing your goals? This is perhaps the most important part of your evaluation and should apply directly to the goals of the student's information product. Consider that this may be included in the product itself as supporting information about the information.

MLA-Style Citation Template:
You want to get all of the information about your resource that you can at one time, so that you don't have to return to locate specifics for your citation or for other reasons. This section provides a template for a standard MLA-style citation. Simply highlight each element (last name, first name, title of the article, date published, etc) and then replace it with the appropriate information from the web page. When you are assembling your information product, all you have to do is copy this citation from your evaluation form and paste it into your product.

Retrieving Information from Web Pages

After we have located information raw materials on the Internet, we must mine them out in ways that take advantage of their digital nature. For instance, simply printing a web page to paper devalues the information because it changes it from bits to atoms. Although there are very good reasons to print a web page, the information is far more valuable if it is harvested into a digital information processing tool such as word processor, graphics program, spreadsheet, or statistics package. The tool that you use depends on the nature and format of the information and your goal for using the information.

Here are instructions for downloading digital information from the Internet and moving it into information processing tools and mediums.

Text to Disk

Objective Task: You have found a web page of which you need the entire text saved to disk. Examples might be the *Declaration of Independence* or *A Tale of Two Cities*. You may be providing disk copies so that your students can easily annotate the document or conduct string searches of the text.

Note: Be aware that when using this technique, you will only be saving the text of the web page. The resulting file will be a text or ASCII file without images and other multimedia.

1. Load the web page into your browser.

2. Pull down the **File** menu and select **Save as...**

3. A standard file dialog box will appear (depending on the operating system: Windows 3.x, 95, or Mac OS). Use the dialog box to find a logical location on your disk to save the file.

Enter a filename for the file with ".txt" as the file
extension. Make sure that the **Save as type:** section is set
to **Plain Text (*.txt)**.

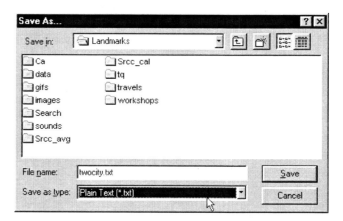

4. Your browser will save the file to the target location on
    your disk as a text file. You should be able to load this
    file into any word processor and most web editors.

Text to Word Processor

Objective Task: You may have found a web page with
information about a historic event, specific location, or scientific
phenomena. In writing a report or preparing a study guide, you
would like to include only portions of the text in your report,
which is being composed with a word processor.

Note: Be aware that when using this technique, you will only be
       saving the text of the web page without images or other
       multimedia.

1. Load the web page into your browser.

2. Using your mouse, highlight the text that you want to
    include in your information product.

3. Pull down the **Edit** menu of your browser and select **Copy**. This will make a copy of the highlighted text, storing the copy in your computers clipboard.

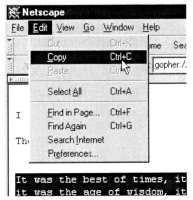

4. Now that your selected text is stored in your computer, you should start your word processor, or other processing tool. If you have already begun work on your information product, move the cursor to the position where you want the web text to be inserted.

5. In your word processor, pull down the **Edit** menu and select **Paste**. This will move the text from your computer's clipboard into the position of the cursor.

Tabular Data to Spreadsheet

Note: There are two techniques for displaying tabular data on a web page, one uses a concept called tables and the other is called preformatted text. If the text is in courier or typewriter looking font and it does not display borders, then it is most likely a preformatted table.

If there are borders around at least some of the cells or if the font is something other than courier, then it is most likely displayed with tables.

Preformatted Tabular Data

These instructions apply to Microsoft Excel. You can also move preformatted tabular data into **Microsoft Works'** spreadsheet for the Macintosh. I have not seen a way for this technique to work on any other spreadsheet program.

1. Load the web page with the tabular data into your browser.

2. Using your mouse, highlight the rows of data that you would like to include in your spreadsheet file.

3. Pull down the **Edit** menu of your browser and select **Copy**. This will make a copy of the highlighted text, storing the data in your computer's clipboard.

4. Start Microsoft Excel and open a new spreadsheet file (or open an existing file in which you want to insert the web data). Select the cell in which you want the top left corner of the data to be stored. Pull down the **Edit** menu and select **Paste**.

5. The data will appear in your spreadsheet. As you examine the affects of pasting the data into the spreadsheet, you will learn that all of it was entered into the column of the cell that you had selected. If you move one cell over to the right into the next column, you will find that it is empty.

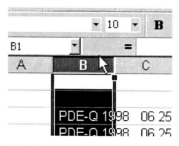

6. To repair this, highlight the entire column that the data flowed into.

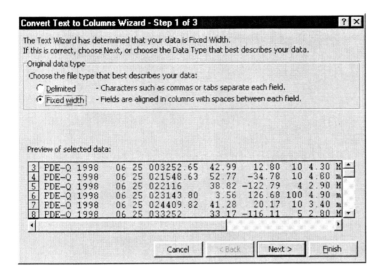

7. When the entire column of the data has been highlighted, pull down the Data menu and select **Text to Columns...** This will produce a wizard or series of dialog boxes that will help you convert your data into a spreadsheet.

8. When the data has been preformatted, the Text to Columns wizard will default to Fixed width. This is good. Click Next to go to the next step.

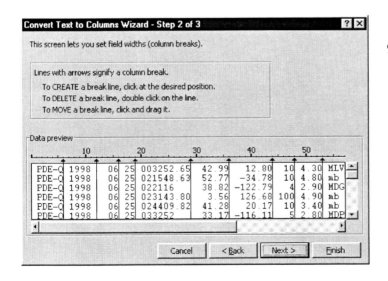

9. In this dialog box, the program makes assumptions about where column divisions should happen. You can add new dividers, move, and delete the dividers that you do not need.

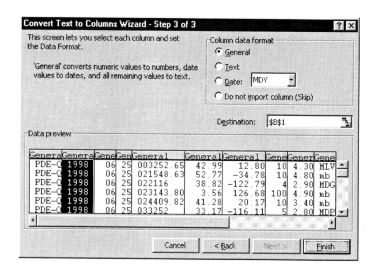

10. This dialog box allows you to determine the type of information for each column. You can designate a column, or combination of columns as **General** or **Numeric Data**, **Text**, or **Date**. In the case of date, you can set the format that you want it converted to. You can also select **Do not import column** to skip the column all together. When you click Finish, you will have a spreadsheet with the data inserted into specific cells.

Tables Formatted Tabular Data

1. Tabular data that has been formatted with table tags must be handled differently from preformatted data. Rather than copying and pasting the data, we must save the entire page. Pull down the File men and select Save as...

A standard file save dialog box will appear. Find a logical target location and be sure that the **Save as type** section is set for text. Then save the file.

2. Next, we have to remove all of the extraneous information, leaving only the data. To do this, load the text file into a text processor, such as WordPad or NotePad. Then carefully delete out all of the information except for the data itself. Then resave the file, with ".txt" as the extension.

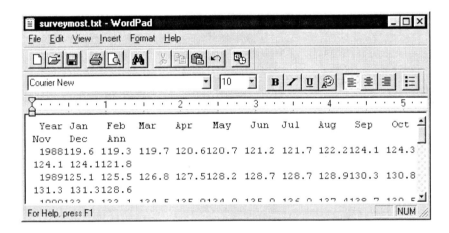

3. Start Microsoft Excel, and open your saved text file. It will automatically open up into the **Text to columns...** wizard. From here, follow the directions beginning with Step 8 above.

Images to Graphics Software

Objective Task: You want your students to learn about specific events that happened in America that led to the Revolutionary War and the Declaration of Independence. To do this, you want to give teams of students a map of Colonial America on disk, so that they can use a graphics program to annotate the map, describing the locations and circumstances of the events. You have found a map on the Web and want to download it to a graphics program.

1. Load the web page into your browser.

2. Using your mouse put the pointer on the image that you want to download. It can be anywhere on the image.

3. If you are using a Windows computer, click the right or secondary mouse button. If you are using a Mac OS computer, hold down the mouse button. After a moment a menu will pop out from the image.

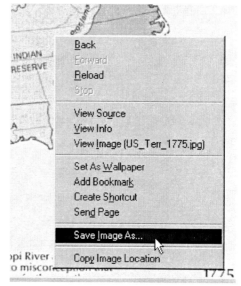

4. From the pop-up menu, select **Save Image As...** A standard file dialog box will appear with which you can select a target location for the file to be saved. The file will either be saved as a GIF or JPeg file. These are the two standard image file types for the World Wide Web.

5. When the file is saved you can open it into your graphics program. If your graphics program will not read GIF or JPeg files, then the file will have to be converted. There are a number of programs available on the Internet that will handle this for you. They range from basic image converters, to full-featured image processing software. Here are some examples and their web locations.

Windows 3.x & 95

LView Pro -- This is a shareware program ($40) that will handle most file type conversions and also includes a variety of image editing features including: filters, cropping, transparent GIF conversion and more.

http://www.lview.com/

Paint Shop Pro -- This shareware ($99) program offers a wide
variety of conversion types, and professional level image
enhancement features including: flexible painting and retouching
brushes, adjustable cropping and selection tools, filters, and many
other enhancement tools.

http://www.jasc.com

Mac OS

GIFConverter -- This is a basic image converter that will take
GIFs and JPegs and turn them into PICT or Paint, which are the
standard image types for the Mac OS environment. The program
is shareware ($30).

http://www.kamit.com/gifconverter.html

GraphicConverter -- This shareware program ($35) does the
same thing as GIFConverter but also has a number of additional
image enhancement features.

http://www.lemkesoft.de/

Retrieving Entire Web Pages and Web Sites

Sometimes bits and pieces of a web site will not serve your
purposes. It is the organization and integration of the entire site
that gives it value to your class. If you know how to write HTML
code, then you can download a site in pieces and then fit it all back
together again, but this is very time consuming.

To save time and avoid having to learn HTML, you need software
that will "harvest" entire web sites. The concept is technically
called "off-line browsing," but what we are talking about doing is
retrieving a page, or series of pages, or an entire site along with its
images and links so that we can view the pages later without being
on the Internet. The concept is frequently called, *whacking* a web

site, because the first program to enter this genre was *Web Whacker* from the **Blue Squirrel**.

It works like this. You load a web page into your favorite browser and decide, for one of several reasons, to download a copy of this page or entire site to diskette. You fire up *Web Whacker* and start a new web group. Then you tell Whacker (click a button) to get the URL from the nearest browser. It grabs the web address of your page and makes itself ready to download. You can then fine tune things by telling it how many levels down to harvest (how many button clicks away from your starting point) and whether you want the files saved by DOS format (eight character filenames with three character extension). Now click **Whack It** and watch it cook.

Web Whacker picks up the HTML files and the images, and recodes the page so that the files can all exist in the same directory. It then picks up the appropriate other HTML files and their graphics, and recodes them. You end up with a file called TOC.HTM, which when you load it into your browser, lists and links to all of the web pages that were harvested into that group.

Again, there are several very good reasons why you would want to harvest a web site:

- You have a computer lab in your school that is networked but not on the Internet. You want your eighth grade social studies class to use a web site on the Civil War. You harvest the site with *Web Whacker* or one of the other harvesting programs, copy the files onto your local area network, install a browser on the computers in the lab and pull the HTML files from the network into each machine's net program. Then bookmark the web site, to make it easier for your students to access the web site.
- You want to preview a web site for your students, but do not have Internet at home. Harvest the site onto a diskette, carry it home and open the pages into your personal computer's browser.
- There is a web site that you want students to use in one of your learning centers. You have a computer in your classroom but no Internet connection. Harvest the site

and run it on your classroom computer for your small groups of students.

- There's a conference coming up and you want to present some innovative design ideas that you have worked into your school's web site. The conference organizers promise a telephone line but you're too smart to depend on it. You harvest your web site onto a disk and bring the disk so that you can display your schools web presence no matter what happens.

Here are several web-harvesting programs that are available for purchase or download.

Web Harvesting Products		
Product	**Company**	**Web site**
Web Whacker	Blue Squirrel	http://www.bluesquirrel.com/whacker/
Web Buddy	DataVis, Inc.	http://www.dataviz.com/dataviz.htm
Teleport Pro	Tennyson Maxwell Information Systems	http://www.tenmax.com/pro.html
NetAttaché Light	Tympani Development, Inc.	http://www.tympani.com/

Issues of Ethics

As you have read the proceeding text, you have probably wondered about this wholesale harvesting, downloading, and whacking of digital property and whether there is anything wrong with doing this. Or perhaps you are a media specialist, and you know that there are considerations that I have not yet made clear.

The answer is, "Yes." When you download information from the Internet, you are taking intellectual property, an information product that was created by somebody. The legalities, at this point are a very hard target to hit, and not being an intellectual property lawyer, I'm not even going to take aim.

I will make two very important recommendations.

1. **Always cite your sources**

2. Always ask permission

Giving credit to the owner or originator of information is courteous, and it is the law -- and it doesn't hurt you one bit. Writing a citation takes about a minute and it extends the information product that you or your students have created by making it a communal work of collaboration -- experts have become partners with you in your work. The *Columbia Guide to Online Style* features information about citing online resources. The URL is:

> http://www.cas.usf.edu/english/walker/mla.html

Asking permission can take a little longer but it too is the courteous thing to do. It is also the law. The *Copyright Law of 1976* included a fair use clause for educators that was hammered out after the law went into affect. The new *Digital Millennium Copyright Act*, which was signed in October of 1998, does not yet have a fair use clause. Therefore, it is required that you have permission from the information source to use it in anyway beyond simply reading it with your web browser.

Even at this, I am not discouraged. Most everyone on the Internet is willing to let teachers and students use their information. You simply need to ask. On the next page is an image of a web page that is designed to help teachers and students seek permission to use web resources for teaching and learning. The page includes the body of a permission requesting e-mail message. You simply fill in the blanks with your specific information, including your e-mail address. After you also enter the e-mail address of the web master or author of the information you want to use, the page will actually send the permission e-mail for you, and the reply will come back to your e-mail address. There are versions of this page for:

- Teachers wanting to use Internet-based information for teaching,
- Teachers who want to harvest an entire web site, and
- A version for students who want to use Internet-based information in their assignments.

The URL of this web page is:

http://landmark-project.com/permission.html

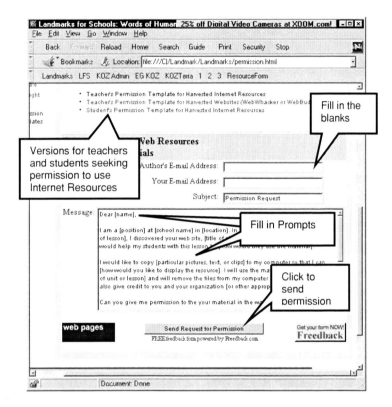

Processing Digital Raw Materials: Instructional Examples

So far in this chapter, we have learned of specific techniques for using the Internet to find, evaluate, credit, and harvest information from the Internet. However, if copying the information and pasting it directly into reports that we or our students would normally do with pencil or typewriter is all that we are going to do with this information, then it is a serious waste of good technology. We would also be missing some interesting teaching and learning opportunities.

Frequently, when I teach workshops for teachers about using the Internet, I ask them to list some of the advantages for using the Internet as a source for information. The answers come easily and usually relate to the:

- Vastness of the Internet,
- The fact that Internet information can be up to date and, at the same time, ancient,
- The wide variety of perspectives that are represented on the Internet
- The fact that information from the Internet can come in a variety of media: text, images, sound, video, animation, etc.

The advantage that is only rarely mentioned is the fact that the information is

Digital

Information found on the Internet comes from a hard disk some place, and you bring it down to your hard disk. This means that the information is suitable to be moved into other information processing tools (as described in the previous pages of this chapter). Once there, you and your students can literately add value to the information: manipulating, adapting, analyzing, and using the information as building blocks for the construction of new, unique, and valuable information products.

By processing digital information with a computer, students become scientists, explorers, and constructors of their own knowledge. Here are just a few ideas on how students can **use** information harvested from the Internet to explore.

Example 1: Teaching the Declaration of Independence

For this scenario, I am going to pretend to be a U.S. history teacher again -- and my class is studying our nation's founding documents. For the next few days we will be studying the *Declaration of Independence*. Although, there is a copy of this document in my students' text books (very fine print), I would like for each student to have his or her own copy on which to take notes.

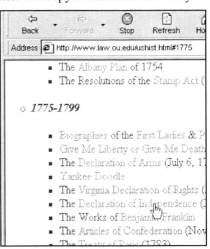

Since the *Declaration of Independence* is a well-known document, I would probably go to a web site called, *A Chronology of US Historical Documents* (http://www.law.ou.edu/ushist.html). This web site features links to more than one hundred historic documents arranged in chronological order. Being a U.S. History teacher, I have this site bookmarked and am there in seconds. I click the link to documents from 1775 to 1799 and our file is number six in the list.

At this point I could easily print the web page. What I really want to do is to better prepare the document for my students. I want them to be able to use it as a tool rather than just text to read. Therefore, I need to be able to format the document -- and using a word processor is just the thing.

My task is to get the text of the *Declaration of Independence* from the web page into my word processor *(see page 130)*. Once the text is in my word processor, I can format the text such that my students can use it as a tool. I want them to be able to add their own comments, notes, impressions, and insights that were drawn from the class discussions and from their own research. One idea might be to double-space the entire document. This would produce space between the lines for comments and other annotations. Another way of formatting the document might be to increase one of the margins by a couple of inches, thereby producing more space for students to include their notes and impressions.

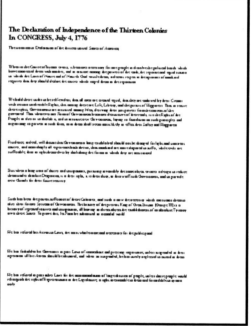

In this example a two-inch margin has been created on the right side and four lines inserted between each paragraph

Example 2: Making History a Science

After spending a few of days researching and discussing our *Declaration of Independence*, I will give my class one more assignment. Each student must read the document one more time, looking for one word in the text that has personal meaning in terms of the goals of America's declaration of independence from

Europe. Students must circle the word that they find, and then fold their paper and place it in their text book. I finally ask the class to meet me in the computer lab tomorrow instead of the classroom.

That evening I return to the Internet and go to a web site called *Landmarks for Schools* (http://www.landmark-project.com). This web site features links to information that can be used by students and teachers as *Raw Materials*. The links are not necessarily educational in nature but are related to content and are frequently primary sources. Once I reach the *Landmarks for Schools* site I click on **The Words of Humankind**. This page includes links to the full text of various documents of Literature, history, and Faith. I move on down to **Words of Power**, where I find a link to a text file entitled, *Inaugural Addresses of Presidents*. This is a single file that includes the full text of all of the Inaugural Addresses of all the Presidents of the United States since George Washington. As an aside, not all of our Presidents actually delivered Inaugural Addresses, but the file is still quite large (900+Kb) owing to the long-windedness of some of our nation's leaders.

Since my browser may not have enough memory to load such a large file, we will download the file directly to disk *(see page 129)*. After I download the file, I copy it over to a diskette and carry it to school the next day. Upon arriving at school, I either install the file on the computer network, or make enough copies of the disk so that small teams of my students can each have a copy.

As my students report to the computer lab, they are either handed a diskette or informed that a file has been stored on the local area network for them. Then I instruct them to load the *Inaugural Addresses* into their word processors and to pull out their copies of the *Declaration of Independence*, locating the word that they circled yesterday, the word that has personal meaning for them. Then I ask them to use the find function of their word processors to find every occurrence of their circled word in the Inaugural Addresses, tracking their word, as a concept, throughout U.S. history. I would then ask each of them to describe to the class, or make a formal oral report, or written report, or conduct even more research creating a web page or other multimedia document that illustrates how their word has evolved during the last 200+ years.

****

Five years ago, a graduate student could not have done this sort of study for anything short of a dissertation. But today, most high school students, using the Internet as their quarry and computers for processing, can seek and discover knowledge rather than simply having to memorize it. Because the information on the Internet is digital, it is a potent raw material for student minds.

Example 3: Searching for Freedom

We are still exploring our nation's founding documents in our U.S. history class. I return to the *Landmarks for* Schools (http://www.landmark-project.com) web site and from the *Words of humankind* section, I download the following documents to disk *(see page 129)*:

- Magna Carta

- Constitution of the Iroquois Nations, 1390

- Mayflower Compact

- American Declaration of Independence

- French Declaration of Rights *(well, it isn't a founding document, but it continues the flow)*

- Emancipation Proclamation

Then I divide my class into groups of three students. In the computer lab, I hand out the diskettes or direct the class to a new folder on the network where each team member is to load two of the files into their word processor. Then I direct each student to use the **Find** function on their word processor to search for every occurrence of the word *free* or any synonyms of the word in both of their documents. They are to then make note of the context of the word, determining its definition in that place in that document.

When the students have finished this part of the activity and printed out their notes, they will meet together again in the classroom where each team will prepare a short presentation on what the concept of freedom meant to the authors of each of the documents. Students should portray how freedom has evolved through history in terms of these major freedom documents.

Example 4: Imports & Exports Activity

Our class, this time, is high school economics. Our students have learned much of the vocabulary and background information involved in its study. Now it is time to start applying their knowledge by discovering the rich interconnectedness of the economic world.

I have decided to conduct a project that will ask students to explore, experiment, and discover economic relationships. The specimen of study will be raw data from the Internet and the laboratory will be the computer. To find this data, our teacher goes back to the Internet, back to the *Landmarks for School* (http://www.landmark-project.com) web site and to a page called *Raw Data*. From this page, the teacher clicks the link for, *Foreign Trade of the U.S. -- From the University of Michigan.*

The page that appears consists of columns and rows of data that depicts the United States' imports and exports from 1961 to 1993. Now given enough time to study our table of data, we might discover some patterns or trends and draw some significant conclusions. However, since this data is *digital*, we can move it into another information processing tool and manipulate the data in some way that will make its understanding more convenient. To do this, we will move the data into a spreadsheet *(see page 131).*

After I captured this data into my spreadsheet, I further format (add value to…) the information by removing all of the columns except for the year and the annual imports and exports. Then I copy the block of data on imports, and paste it next to the data on exports so that the years line up. We now have an effective table of data that provides a comparison of imports and exports for the United States from 1961 to 1993.

As class starts, our teacher divides her students into groups of three or four students each. She explains that they are going to be researching a question that they themselves will be asking. Using a computer and projector (or transparency that was printed from the computer screen) the class sees the actual data file. After explaining what the data represents, the teacher uses the spreadsheet program to convert the data into a graph.

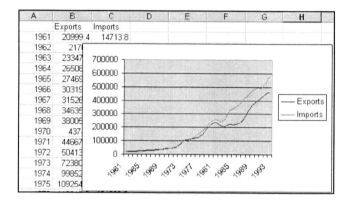

After some discussion, the class will ask about the split that seemed to occur between imports and exports during the early 1980s. The teacher then asks each team to take a look at historic events during the early 1980s to determine the events and conditions that may have lead to the observed split.

Example 5: Tracking Earthquakes

My science class is studying seismology. We have been discussing the tectonic plates and are beginning a more in-depth look at earthquakes. I go to my web browser and pull up a web site called the *National Earthquake Information Center* from the *U.S. Geologic Survey*.

http://wwwneic.cr.usgs.gov/neis/epic/epic_global.html

This web page features a search engine that allows us to search their database of earthquake records going back thousands of years BC. We decide to use only recent earthquakes so I click the appropriate radio button for the **Most Recent Events (1998 05 28 - 1998 07 25)**. Then I click **Submit Search**.

After a moment I receive a web page that lists statistical information on earthquakes from around the world that have occurred between the dates of 5/28/98 and 7/25/98. The table of data includes among other things the year, month, day and time. It

also includes longitude and latitude, magnitude, and depth at the
epicenter. I copy the table of data and paste it into a Microsoft
Excel file *(see page 131)*. Then I convert the pasted column into a
breakout of columns, importing only the longitude and latitude.

This web site automatically reports longitudes to the west of the
Prime Meridian and south of the Equator as negative numbers.
Some web site report this in the traditional way as 107W, or 107
degrees west of the Prime Meridian. To plot these points I would
have to convert these listings to positive negative numbers by
creating two new columns where I would add the following
formula

	A	B	C	D	E	F
1	-72.54	W	-17.18	S	=if(B1="W",A1*-1,A1)	=if(D1="S",B1*-1,B1)
2	116.14	E	-1.53	S	=if(B2="W",A2*-1,A2)	=if(D2="S",B2*-1,B2)
3	-122.81	W	38.81	N	=if(B3="W",A3*-1,A3)	=if(D3="S",B3*-1,B3)

The formula in cell E1 reads:

> If the content of cell B1 is "W", then multiply the contents
> of A1 times -1. This converts the number to a negative
> integer. Then place the resulting value in this cell -- E1.
> If B1 is not "W" then simply place the contents of A1 into
> cell E1.

The results are:

	A	B	C	D	E	F
1	72.54	W	17.18	S	-72.54	-17.18
2	116.14	E	1.53	S	116.14	-1.53
3	122.81	W	38.81	N	-122.81	38.81

Then I highlight the latitude and longitude columns and click the graph tool in Excel and pick a scatter plot graph. What do you think the resulting graph looks like? Try it and see!

Example 6: The Geography of Historic Events

We are back in history class where we are studying significant events of the 1960s. In preparation for a lesson, I go to a web site called *The TerraServer* (http://www.terraserver.com). This site holds an archive of satellite images from around the world. *The TerraServer* will soon represent the largest online database in the world.

Since *TerraServer* will not show me a satellite image based on an address, I create a new web browser window and go to another web site called *Map Blast* (http://www.mapblast.com). Similar to *Map Quest* (http://www.mapquest.com), *Map Blast* has one unique feature. When you enter an address, it produces a street map of the area, like *Map Quest* and many other similar services, but it also gives you the longitude and latitude of the location.

I enter *100 Elm Street, Dallas Texas* into *Map Blast*. After a moment, I see a map of the area, and beneath the map I copy the map coordinates (longitude and latitude) and pass them into *The TerraServer* and click **Search**. After a moment, *TerraServer* produces a satellite image of Dallas, Texas. The resolution is eight meters to the pixel. Still I recognize the neighborhood that I am interested in. I click the neighborhood and after a moment a new image appears set to eight meters to the pixel. Clicking one more time on the neighborhood and receive an image with a resolution of 1.5 meters to the pixel.

Satellite Image of Elm Street, Dallas Texas at 1.5 meters per pixel

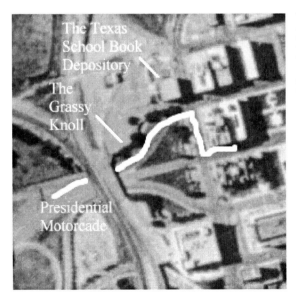

When the new satellite image is loaded I harvest it and move it into a graphics program *(see page 135)*. Now I can annotate the image for use in describing the assassination of President John Kennedy.

---

* Printed with permission from *Aerial Images, Inc.* and *SOVINFORMSPUTNIK*

Some Raw Data Resources

Following are several raw data resources on the Internet that can be used as teaching and learning raw materials. Beneath each resource is a suggestion of how it might be used for teaching or learning.

Service	Description/URL/Publisher
- Air Pollution Monitors Database	"This is a very powerful database of historic air pollution levels that can be accessed by state, county or city. Each report can be converted to TAB or COMMA delimited files for importing into spreadsheet programs." http://www.epa.gov/airsweb/monreps.htm U.S. Environmental Protection Agency

Application: *Combine state air pollution data with population density data on a spreadsheet and have student plot graphs to identify correlations. Then have students work in teams to speculate on reasons for the patterns and reasons for the states that deviate from the patterns.*

Service	Description/URL/Publisher
- Bureau of Labor Statistics Data	Many statistics on U.S. labor. http://stats.bls.gov:80/datahome.htm Bureau of Labor Statistics

Application: *Divide students into teams with each team responsible for a region of the U.S. Have each team harvest unemployment data on each state in their region and plot a comparison between each state and the U.S. unemployment rate. Ask each team to identify the state that performs the best and the state that performs the least satisfactorily in comparison with the national rate. Then ask each team to research the state with the lowest employment rate and suggest an industry that might be ideally introduced to improve the employment rate.*

Service	Description/URL/Publisher
- Current Data & Forecasts	A clickable U.S. map that returns the day's weather conditions progressing through the day and a two-day forecast. http://wxp.atms.purdue.edu/interact.html Purdue University

Application: *The data in this service represents moderate to large cities, and each city includes its map coordinates. Students might pick 20 cities across the country representing different longitudes and latitudes. Then over a period of time they might collect daily weather data and record it by map position on a spreadsheet. Students could then plot the data on a graph to attempt to identify weather patterns by region of the U.S.*

- Food Finder

A searchable database of nutritional characteristics of individual meals from the leading fast food restaurants. You enter the restaurant and the meal and you get the data.

http://www.olen.com/food/
Olen Publishing

Application: *Students can access data on the nutritional characteristics of specific foods at different fast food restaurants and record the data on a spreadsheet. Then they can work in teams to identify the most nutritious restaurant or the most nutritious mean compiled from all of the fast food stops.*

- Historic Climate Data for the Southeastern United States

"You choose the state and then the city and then you get the average maximum, average mean, average minimum, high maximum, low maximum, high mean, etc temperature for each day of the year over the past fifty years in most cases."

http://water.dnr.state.sc.us/climate/sercc/climate_calendars.html
South Carolina Department of Natural Resources

Application: *If your class is in the Southeastern part of the U.S., you can find your town, and then plot each day's temp and precipitation along with the statistical data available through this site to visualize through graphs how this years weather compares with the historic averages, highs, and lows.*

- Interstate Commodity Shipments

You get a map of the United States. Click on a state and you get another map of the U.S. with states color coded by the weight or value of commodities shipped there from the originating state. There are also supporting tables of data.

http://www.bts.gov/gis/maps/inter/index.html
U.S. Department of Transportation

Application: 1. *Students, working in teams, can identify the state to which their state sells the most goods. Then they can describe how they might improve transportation to those states and make a presentation to the class*
2. *Students, working in teams, can identify states to which their state does not deliver many goods. Then they can research those states and speculate on industries that might be added to their state to better server the under-served states. Then make a presentation to the class.*

Some "Words of Humankind" Resources

Following are several "Words of Humankind" resources on the Internet that can be used as teaching and learning raw materials. Beneath each resource is a suggestion of how it might be used for teaching or learning.

Service	Description/URL/Publisher
- Biographical Dictionary	This is a database of biographical information on famous and infamous people. It includes an alphabetical listing and a searchable index. Brought to us by the TV program, Biography. http://www.biography.com/find/find.html A&E Television Networks

Application: *This sort of resource is the reason you need a computer in your classroom that is connected to the Internet. On those occasions that you are discussing some historic period or event, and students ask detailed questions about the people who lived and contributed at that time, this becomes the place to go for answers on the web.*

Service	Description/URL/Publisher
- "California as I Saw It:" First-Person Narratives of California's Early Years, 1849-1900	Consists of the full texts and illustrations of 190 works documenting the formative era of California's history through eyewitness accounts. http://memory.loc.gov/ammem/cbhtml/cbhome.html The Library of Congress

Application: *As students are studying the westward movement, they might create a read through many of the narratives and then create a weekly newspaper, reporting the common and uncommon occurrences in California during it's early years.*

Service	Description/URL/Publisher
- Chief Joseph Speaks	This web page includes selected statements and speeches of Joseph, Chief of the Nez Perce. http://www3.pbs.org/weta/thewest/wpages/wpgs660/jospeak.htm PBS

Application: *A team of students might include the recitation of these words as part of a multimedia presentation on the U.S. treatment of Native Americans during the 1800s.*

Service	Description/URL/Publisher
- Electronic Text Center -- Latin	An extensive selection of German literature. http://etext.lib.virginia.edu/lat-on.html University of Virginia Library

Service	Description/URL/Publisher
- Excepts from Slave Narratives	This is a rich and interesting site that features primary sources on conditions of slaves prior to 1880. Http://vi.uh.edu/pages/mintz/primary.htm Steven Mintz

Application: *These texts can be used as part of a multimedia presentation on slavery in the U.S. Students might even record their recitation of the narratives and include them as audio files.*

Service	Description/URL/Publisher
- Gold Rush Memoir	This is the full text of memoirs written by Eugene Ring about his experiences during the California gold rush. http://uts.cc.utexas.edu/~scring/index.html Steven Charles Ring

Application: *Have students read the words of Eugene Ring. Then ask them to pretend that they are Mr. Ring, and write several letters home to the East, describing his experiences to his family.*

Service	Description/URL/Publisher
- Historical Text Archives	"This web site features text archives and other resources on more obscure facets of U.S. history, including: Yorktown, pre-1700 documents, Georgia before Oglethorpe, and northwest coast indian history" http://www.msstate.edu/Archives/History/USA/colonial/colonial.html Mississippi State University

Application: *One of the links on this site points to fashions of the 17th century. Students might harvest images of cloths people wore during this time and make a multimedia presentation (PowerPoint, HyperStudio, or a web site)*

Service	Description/URL/Publisher
- Project Gutenberg	Project Gutenberg was the first to begin digitizing the great works of civilization. It began work in 1971 to enter texts into computers and then eventually to make them available via FTP, the Gopher, and now the Web. http://promo.net/pg/ Michael Hart

Application: *Teachers can download the complete texts of literature that their students are reading. After the books or plays are read, students can use the disk versions and word processor to research the texts, searching for occurrences of specific keywords. Students can also look for patterns of word or phrase usage or commonly used metaphors and other literary techniques.*

-	The Complete Works of William Shakespeare	This site provides access to all of the published works of the Bard. The plays are hyperlinked to a Shakespeare dictionary where unfamiliar words can be clicked for their meaning. http://the-tech.mit.edu/Shakespeare/works.html MIT

Application: *Shakespeare is perhaps the most quoted writer in history. The next time you are introducing a topic to your class, go to this site and search the entire works of the Bard for occurrences of keywords related to the topic. You may find a fine quote with which to dazzle your class.*

Self-Expression

As teachers, we know how well we learn things when we have to teach them. We know that we learn things more powerfully when we must plan, organize and express information to other people with a goal in mind. As teachers, we know this especially well, because this is the nature of our job -- planning, organizing, and expressing information to other people such that our audience understands and learns it. No one knows the content of any topic better than someone who teaches it does.

Leveraging this sense of was the first educational application of e-mail. During the middle 1980s, teachers in California used e-mail to provided their students with real audiences for their writings. The idea was to promote better writing and to improve the retention of content.

Margaret Riel and Moshe Cohen wrote that

Writing is a communicative act, a way of sharing observations, information, thoughts or ideas with ourselves and others. Writing is usually directed to a person or persons for a specific purpose.

They continue to reveal that most writing in the classroom is *decontextualized*, or the context becomes writing for a grade. When comparing 7th graders' writing quality when working for a grade, and the quality of their writing when the audience was other 7th graders in another part of the world, Riel and Cohen found that students:

- Wrote more,
- In greater detail,
- Taking greater care with grammar,
- Punctuation and
- Spelling.[*]

When the World Wide Web appeared, and these same teachers discovered how easy it was to create web pages, students around the world started publishing to global audiences through the web. Not only were they learning better sentence structure, but they were having to organize their ideas in more powerful ways in order to establish logical hyperlinks between concepts.

On the next page is an example of a project that students might engage in that includes all three of the processes described in our earlier discussions for using information raw materials:

Mining the Internet for information raw materials

Processing those raw materials using information processing software

Producing and publishing a new information product

---

[*] Cohen, Moshe. Riel, Margaret. The Effect of Distant Audiences on Students' Writing *American Educational Research Journal*; v26 n2 (Sum 1989): 143-59.

Assignment

1. **Ask your students to take a virtual field trip to Mars.**

2. Ask your students to research the Internet for information about the planet Mars and to collect information that they find including text, images, animations, video clips, etc.

3. Tell your students that they are to create a report on their fieldtrip, describing in as much detail as they can what they saw when they took their trip -- pretending that the class actually traveled to the red planet.

4. The assignment can be to write a paper report, a multimedia presentation, or a web page.

The example on the next page is a web page created for this assignment.

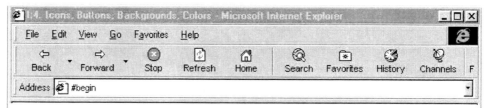

Our Day on Mars

When we landed on Mars, early in the Martian morning, it was very cold. It can get as cold as 190 degrees below zero, Fahrenheit. We knew that it could get warmer since Mars can get as hot as 98 degrees. We also had to bundle up for other reasons. Since 95% of the atmosphere of Mars is carbon dioxide, we need helmets and oxygen to breath.[1]. Here is a picture of the Martian sunrise that we saw shortly after landing.[2]

When it got warm enough, we boarded our super fast surface skimmer to visit some of the historic sites on Mars. We saw the Mariner 4   spacecraft which landed on the planet in 1965, both Viking landers in 1976, and the Pathfinder which landed July 4, 1997. We also visited the Olympus Mons, which is the largest mountain in the Solar System. It is 78,000 feet tall.[3]

It was really quite windy during the afternoon. There was a great deal of dust in the air. In our super fast surface skimmer, we visited a region of Mars that has lots of sand dunes. They looked very much like the dunes of Earth.[4]

 Later on in the afternoon, Timothy found what he thought was a Martian skateboard. It turned out to be the Sojourner Rover, which was a Martian experiment in itself. Scientists wanted to learn about creating robotic rovers for Mars so that more effective units could be built and used in the future to collect information about the red planet.[5]

When we took off from Mars, it was quite a ride. We had to go 5,000 meters per second to break free of the planet's gravity.[1]

Here are some links to some web pages about Mars:

- Mars the Red Planet
- Mars Exploration
- Mars [Nine Planets]
- Mars [NASA]

1   California Institute of Technology. "Mars." Welcome to the Planets. November 20, 1995.
     http://pds.jpl.nasa.gov/planets/welcome/mars.htm (July 1, 1998).
2   "Exploring Mars." Version or File Number, if applicable. February, 1998.
     http://www.exploringmars.org/images/pathfinder.html (July 1, 1998).
3   National Air and Space Museum. "The Surface of Mars." Mars: The Red Planet. . 1997.
     http://ceps.nasm.edu:2020/ETP/MARS/SURFACE/wind.html (July 2, 1998).

Web Publishing

The web page on the previous page was produced using a language called HTML (HyperText Markup Language). It is a set of tags that are inserted into the text of the report to control the layout and behavior of a web page.

Here is the HTML code (with explanations) that produced the web page on the previous page. Do not let this example scare you. HTML is much simpler than it looks. Many of your students may already be doing this. There is a more complete and organized HTML reference guide on page 164.

Code	Comments
`<HTML>`	Starts web document

`<HEAD>`
`  <TITLE>A Trip to Mars</TITLE>`
`</HEAD>`
	Head section of the document. The text between the *title* tags appears in the titlebar of the browser.

`<BODY BGCOLOR="#ffffff">`	Starts the body of the document. The *bgcolor* attribute makes the background color of the document white.
`<H1>Our Day on Mars</H1>`	Makes the heading large and bold.
`<IMG SRC="bluefade.gif" WIDTH="100%"> `	The long blue border beneath the head. The *br* tag forces a line break.
`When we landed on Mars, early in the Martian morning, it was very cold. It can get as cold as 190 degrees below zero, Fahrenheit. We knew that it could get warmer since Mars can get as hot as 98 degrees. We also had to bundle up for other reasons. Since 95% of the atmosphere of Mars is carbon dioxide, we need`	First Paragraph: The *SUP* tags cause the footnote markers to be elevated.

```
helmets and oxygen to breath.<SUP><A
HREF="#1">1</A></SUP>. Here is a picture of the
Martian sunrise that we saw shortly after
landing.<SUP><A HREF="#2">2</A></SUP>
<P>
```

The *<A HREF="#2">2</a>* hyperlinks the number 2 footnote marker to the number 2 footnote at the bottom of the page.

```
<IMG SRC="olympus.gif" WIDTH="107" HEIGHT="100"
ALIGN="Right">
<IMG SRC="sol24_sunrise_s.gif" WIDTH="300"
HEIGHT="82" ALIGN="Right">
```

The *IMG* tags display two pictures. The *WIDTH & HEIGHT* attributes set the size of the images and the *ALIGN* attribute align the images to the right.

Second Paragraph:

```
When it got warm enough, we boarded our super fast
surface skimmer to visit some of the historic sites
on Mars. We saw the Mariner 4 spacecraft which landed
on the planet in 1965, both Viking landers in 1976,
and the Pathfinder which landed July 4, 1997. We also
visited the Olympus Mons, which is the largest
mountain in the Solar System. It is 78,000 feet
tall.<SUP><A HREF="#3">3</A></SUP>
<P>
```

Third Paragraph

```
It was really quite windy during the afternoon. There
was a great deal of dust in the air. In our super
fast surface skimmer, we visited a region of Mars
that has lots of sand dunes. They looked very much
like the dunes of Earth.<SUP><A HREF="#4">4</A></SUP>
<P>
```

```
<IMG SRC="sojourner.gif" WIDTH="135" HEIGHT="164"
ALIGN="Left">
```

The *IMG* tag and associated attributes set the size and alignment of the rover picture.

Fourth Paragraph

```
Later on in the afternoon, Timothy found what he
thought was a Martian skateboard. It turned out to be
the Sojourner Rover, which was a Martian experiment
in itself. Scientists wanted to learn about creating
robotic rovers for Mars so that more effective units
```

could be built and used in the future to collect
information about the red planet.<SUP><A
HREF="#5">5</A></SUP>
<P>
When we took off from Mars, it was quite a ride. We
had to go 5,000 meters per second to break free of
the planet's gravity.^{<A HREF="#1">1</A>}

<H3>Here are some links to some web pages about
Mars:</H3>

<UL>
<LI>
<A HREF="http://ceps.nasm.edu:2020/MARS/MARS.html">
Mars the Red Planet</A>
<LI>
<A HREF="http://fys.ku.dk/~stubbe/folder/folder.htm">
Mars Exploration</A>
<LI>
<A HREF="http://seds.lpl.arizona.edu/nineplanets/
nineplanets/mars.html">Mars [Nine Planets]</A>
<LI>
<A HREF="http://pds.jpl.nasa.gov/planets/welcome/
mars.htm">Mars [NASA]</A>
<LI>
<A HREF="http://www-mgcm.arc.nasa.gov/">Mars
Today</A>
</UL>
<P>
   <HR>
<P>

<TABLE BORDER="0" CELLPADDING="2">

   <TR VALIGN="Top">
      <TD><A NAME="1"><SMALL>1</SMALL></A></TD>
      <TD><SMALL>California Institute of Technology.
"Mars." Welcome to the Planets. November 20, 1995.
http://pds.jpl.nasa.gov/planets/welcome/mars.htm
(July1, 1998).</SMALL></TD>
   </TR>

   <TR VALIGN="Top">
      <TD><A NAME="2"><SMALL>2</SMALL></A></TD>
      <TD><SMALL>"Exploring Mars." Version or File
Number, if applicable. February, 1998.
http://www.exploringmars.org/images/pathfinder.html

Fifty Paragraph

Heading tags
make the head
larger and more
bold.
The *UL & LI* tags
produce a
bulleted or
Unordered List.
The *A* tags with
HREF attributes
establish
hyperlinks to
other web sites.

The *HR* tag
produces a
horizontal rule or
line.
The *TABLE*, *TR*,
and *TD* tags form
a table that houses
the citations and
their reference
numbers.

```
(July 1, 1998).</SMALL></TD>
  </TR>

  <TR VALIGN="Top">
  <TD><A NAME="3"><SMALL>4</SMALL></A></TD>
  <TD><SMALL>National Air and Space Museum. "The
Surface of Mars." Mars: The Red Planet. . 1997.
http://ceps.nasm.edu:2020/ETP/MARS/SURFACE/wind.html
(July 2, 1998).</SMALL></TD>
  </TR>

</TABLE>

</BODY>

</HTML>
```

`</BODY>`	Ends the body of the document.
`</HTML>`	Ends the HTML document.

Basic HTML Reference Guide

When you get accustomed to the process of coding documents for the World Wide Web, it is only a matter of having access to the codes and what they accomplish. There are a variety of documents on the Internet that will serve as excellent references. Some of them are:

HTML Reference Manual, from Sandia National Laboratories	http://www.sandia.gov/sci_compute/html_ref.html
Compendium of HTML Elements, by Ron Woodall	http://www.htmlcompendium.org/index.htm
HTML Quick Reference, from the University of Kansas	http://www.cc.ukans.edu/~acs/docs/other/HTML_quick.shtml

Here is a reference table for basic HTML codes with examples. In this reference document, all tags are in plain text, Arial font. The examples of content will be italicized. Also, the use of indenting is strictly for the benefit of the person who is reading the code. Indenting certain programming codes is a very useful practice as it allows the programmer to make the relationships between hierarchical codes clear. It gives a visual sense of the structure of the program. For instance, indenting the <LI> tags inside of the <UL> tags give a visual sense that the <LI>s belong to the <UL>.

```
<UL>
    <LI> Item one</LI>
    <LI> Item two</LI>
    <LI> Item three</LI>
</UL>
```

Since the Internet ignores all excessive spaces and carriage returns, it ignores the spaces that you use to indent certain tags.

Tag Structure

Most HTML codes, or tags, tell your web browser to start doing something to the following text. Then another tag tells it when to stop. Although this is not the case with all tags, it is the convention that is consistent with a vast majority of HTML. For instance, let's say that you want the name of your school to be in bold text.

> This is the web page for **Earl Bradsher Elementary School**, in Roxboro, North Carolina.

You will need a tag that tells your reader's web browser to start making the text bold at the word *Earl*. Then you will need another tag that tells it to stop bolding the text after the word *School*. There are two things to understand about tags in order to format the sentence above and to accomplish most web page coding.

1. All tags are enclosed by angle brackets or greater-than and less-than symbols. The tag that causes text to be bolded is:

2. Ending tags look exactly like the beginning tag except that the tag's code (b) is preceded by a forward slash (/). So the tag that ends the bolding format is:

Consequently, to code the sentence above so that Earl Bradsher Elementary School is bold, the sentence would be written like this:

This is the web page for Earl Bradsher Elementary School, in Roxboro, North Carolina.

Document Structure

There are a number of tags that are common to all HTML or web documents. They structure the document into the HEAD and BODY sections, as we did in the virtual fieldtrip page. This diagram explains how these tags are structured.

```
<HTML>
```

`<HEAD>`
  `<TITLE>`
Kennedy Elementary School Home Page
  `</TITLE>`
`</HEAD>`
	Information about the document -- usually only the TITLE -- appears between the HEAD tags.	The Entire HTML docu ment lies betwe en the HTML tags.

`<BODY>`
The text, images, and hyperlinks of the document. What you want people to read.
`</BODY>`
	The content of the document -- what appears on the screen -- lies between the BODY tags.	

```
</HTML>
```

The following pages describe commonly used HTML tags with examples.

An HTML Reference

Tags	Examples
Headings	

<h3>Technology in Schools**</h3>** Technology in schools holds great potential for empowering teachers to create more dynamic and effective learning environments. But a crucial factor in the successful use of technology in schools is teacher staff development...

Technology in Schools

Technology in schools holds great potential for empowering teachers to create more dynamic and effective learning environments. But a crucial factor in the successful use of technology in schools is teacher staff development...

Note: The number in the *heading* tag indicates the size of the heading text. One (1) is the largest and six (6) the smallest.

Internet Heading
<h1>...</h1>

Internet Heading
<h2>...</h2>

Internet Heading
<h3>...</h3>

Internet Heading
<h4>...</h4>

Internet Heading
<h5>...</h5>

Internet Heading
<h6>...</h6>

Bold

With sufficiently powerful computers, classrooms can be turned into ****learning laboratories**** where students learn through exploration and experimentation.

With sufficiently powerful computers, classrooms can be turned into **learning laboratories** where students learn through exploration and experimentation.

Italics

The **<i>**Library of Congress**</i>** provides valuable information for teachers through its Internet World Wide Web site.

The *Library of Congress* provides valuable information for teachers through its Internet World Wide Web site.

Note: This tag should be used sparingly since some monitors do not display italics very effectively.

Tags	Examples

Underline

A teacher in Virginia found that her students produced better reports on the book, **<u>**Moby Dick**</u>**, when they had access to a disk copy of the full text that had been downloaded from the Internet.

A teacher in Virginia found that her students produced better reports on the book, <u>Moby Dick</u>, when they had access to a disk copy of the full text that had been downloaded from the Internet.

Paragraph Break

<p>...it is difficult for students in most schools to have access to the Internet since there is usually only one Internet computer in the whole building.**</p>** **<p>**However, that one computer can still be used as a professional resource by teachers in a wide variety of ways. **</p>**

...it is difficult for students in most schools to have access to the Internet since there is usually only one Internet computer in the whole building.

However, that one computer can still be used as a professional resource by teachers in a wide variety of ways.

Note: An attribute can be added to the <p> tag that will align the paragraph to the left, right, or center.

    <p align=left>   Left aligned paragraph
    <p align=right>   Right aligned paragraph
    <p align=center>   Centered paragraph

Line Break

Modem:**
**A device for connecting computers together over phone lines.

Modem:
A device for connecting computers together over phone lines.

Lists

Components of a dialup Internet Station:
<ul>
  <li>Computer
  <li>Software
  <li>Phone Line
  <li>Modem
  <li>Service Provider
</ul><p>
Process for getting into the World Wide

Components of a dialup Internet Station:

- Computer
- Software
- Phone Line
- Modem
- Service Provider

Process for getting into the World Wide

Web:
```
<ol>
  <li>Run your PPP or SLIP software to
open a connect.
  <li>Quit your PPP or SLIP software.
  <li>Run your web browser software.  It
should open up to your home page on
the Internet.
</ol>
```

Web:

1. Run your PPP or SLIP software to
    open a connect.
2. Quit your PPP or SLIP software.
3. Run your web browser software. It
    should open up to your home page on
    the Internet.

Horizontal Rules (lines)

```
<h3>Options</h3>
<hr>
```
Your options are to:
```
<hr width=70%>
```
Use FTP to download and upload software
through the Internet
```
<hr width=60%>
```
Use Gopher to navigate the Internet via
menus
```
<hr width=50%>
```
Use the World Wide Web to utilize a
hypertext feature in information
```
<hr width=40%>
```
Or chat with people through chat rooms or
virtual environments.`<p>`

Options

Your options are to:

Use FTP to download and upload
software through the Internet

Use Gopher to navigate the Internet
via menus

Use the World Wide Web to utilize a
hypertext feature in information

Or chat with people through chat rooms
or virtual environments.

Font Formats

`<font size=5>`T`</font>`he most
important tool for teachers as they
integrate technology into their
curriculums is their imaginations.

`<font face=arial size=1>`The most
important tool for teachers as they
integrate technology into their
curriculums is their imaginations. `</font>`

The most important tool for teachers
as they integrate technology into
their curriculums is their
imaginations.

The most important tool for teachers as they
integrate technology into their curriculums is
their imaginations.

<font color=" #808080">The most important tool for teachers as they integrate technology into their curriculums is their imaginations. **</font>**

The most important tool for teachers as they integrate technology into their curriculums is their imaginations.

Note: The color code, #808080, represents dark gray. There are 256 such codes that represent each of 256 different colors from #FFFFFF producing white to #000000 producing black.

Hyperlinks

Click **<a href="ss.html">**Social Studies**</a>** to access resources on maps.

Click Social Studies to access resources on maps.

Note: The text within the beginning <a> tag and the ending </a> tag will become a hyperlink. When clicked on, the page will be replaced with the web page file, ss.html.

Graphics & Clickable Images

The graphic file is called, netday.gif, and is in a subdirectory called "images".
3.

```
<center>
 <a href="netday96.html">
 <img src="/images/netday.gif"
 border=0>
 </a>
Click this button
</center>
```
4.

Click this button

Note: If the "border=0" is left out, a hyperline (blue) border will appear around the graphic image.

An alternative to manually typing all of the HTML tags into the document is to use a web editor program. They offer several advantage over typing the code in, including the fact that you do not have to know all of the codes. By simply highlighting the text that you want to format and then pulling down the **Format** menu and selecting the formatting feature you want to employ, the program inserts the appropriate tags around the highlighted text.

Other web editors fall under the category commonly called "WYSIWYG," pronounced:

wizy-wig

WYSIWYG is an acronym for:

What You See Is What You Get

Using a WYSIWYG web editor is more like using a word processor than writing computer code. You layout the page and format the text and images in much the say way that you would create a word-processed document. The program inserts the appropriate HTML codes in the background. When you save the file, it is saved as a text, HTML file.

It is important to be cautious with WYSIWYG programs since they are not perfect. Frequently, a web page will have the look that you are trying to produce while in the editor, but when you load it into a browser, like Netscape Navigator, the page turns into alphabet soup. It is just as important to constantly test your pages with a browser when using WYSIWYG editors as it is when using a code editor.

On the next page are some web editors that are commonly used by educators. The WYSIWYG editors are marked with an asterisk (*).

Software	Platform	URL	WYSIWYG	Approx. Cost
AOLPress	Win3.1 Win95 MacOS	http://www.aolpress.com	*	Free
Claris HomePage	Win95 MacOS	http://www.claris.com/products/homepage3.html	*	$79.95 to $99.95
Microsoft FrontPage	Win95 MacOS	http://www.microsoft.com/frontpage/	*	$119.99 to $139.99
HTML Web Weaver Lite	MacOS Shareware	http://www.miracleinc.com/		$25.00
Page Spinner	MacOS Shareware	http://www.optima-system.com/pagespinner/		$25.00
Arachnophilia	Win95	http://www.arachnoid.com/		Free
CoffeeCup HTML Editor++ Pro	Win95 Shareware	http://www.coffeecup.com/editor		$40.00
Netscape Composer	Win95 MacOS	http://www.netscape.com Comes with Netscape Communicator	*	Free
Microsoft FrontPage Express	Win95 MacOS	http://www.microsoft.com Comes with a full installation of Microsoft Internet Explorer	*	Free

One of the most amazing editors in the list above is AOL Press. This program was provided to AOL customers as a tool for creating web pages, but it is also available to non-customers. This program has three important features that need to be mentioned.

1. AOL Press is free! You can download this program from the Internet and install it on every computer in your school. There is a version for Windows 3.x, a version for Windows 95/98, and a version for the MacOS.

2. AOL Press includes a 100+ page manual and tutorial that can either be read online, or downloaded as an Acrobat (.pdf) file.

3.   AOL Press is a fine web editing program that features both WYSIWYG and code editing. The interface is good with a customizable tool bar.

The next page features the same web page report on Mars, but with tips on how to employ the various formatting options with AOL Press.

Make the title text large and bold:

1. Highlight the text with your mouse.
2. Pull down the "Format" menu then select "heading" and then "Hdg2" from the pop-out menu.

Adding an Image:

1. Place the cursor at the position of the image.
2. Click the "Insert image" button.
3. Click the "Browse" button and find the filename of the image file and select it.
4. Click "OK"
5. In the "Alignment section, click "Left"

This causes the image to align to the left, forcing text to wrap around to the right.

6. Click "OK" again.

Create a bulleted List:

1. Highlight the items to be bulleted.
2. Click the "Bulleted list" button.

Create a link anchor:

1. Highlight the text that is to be the anchor.
2. Pull down the "Element" menu and select "Anchor".
3. Enter an anchor name or leave the one that is entered for you.
4. Click "OK".

Our Day on Mars

When we landed on Mars, early in the Martian morning, it was very cold. It can get as cold as 190 degrees below zero, Fahrenheit. We knew

that it could get warmer since Mars can get as hot as 98 degrees. We also had to bundle up for other reasons. Since 95% of the atmosphere of Mars is carbon dioxide, we need helmets and oxygen to breath.[1] Here is a picture of the Martian sunrise that we saw shortly after landing.[2]

When it got warm enough, we boarded our super fast surface skimmer to visit some of the historic sites on Mars. We saw the Mariner 4 spacecraft which landed on the planet in 1965, both Viking landers in 1976, and the Pathfinder which landed July 4, 1997. We also visited the Olympus Mons, which is the largest mountain in the Solar System. It is 78,000 feet tall.[3]

It was really quite windy during the afternoon. There was a great deal of dust in the air. In our super fast surface skimmer, we visited a region of Mars that has lots of sand dunes. They looked very much like the dunes of Earth.[4]

 Later on in the afternoon, Timothy found what he thought was a Martian skateboard. It turned out to be the Sojourner Rover, which was a Martian experiment in itself. Scientists wanted to learn about creating robotic rovers for Mars so that more effective units could be built and used in the future to collect information about the red planet.[5]

When we took off from Mars, it was quite a ride. We had to go 5,000 meters per second to break free of the planet's gravity.[1]

Here are some links to some web pages about Mars:

- Mars the Red Planet
- Mars Exploration
- Mars [Nine Planets]
- Mars [NASA]
- Mars Today

1 California Institute of Technology. Mars. Welcome to the Planets. November 20, 1995. http://pds.jpl.nasa.gov/planets/welcome/mars.htm (July1, 1998).
2 "Exploring Mars." Version or File Number, if applicable. February, 1998. http://www.exploringmars.org/image/pathfinder.html (July 1, 1998).
3 Author's last name, first name. "Document name." Title of Complete Work (if applicable). Version or File Number, if applicable. Document date or date of last revision (if different from access date). Protocol and address, access path or directories (date of access).
4 National Air and Space Museum. The Surface of Mars. Mars. The Red Planet. . 1997. http://ceps.nasa.edu:2020/ETPMARS/SURFACE/mrsd.html (July 2, 1998).
5 Jet Propulsion Laboratory 'Rover Sojourner. Mission Overview.' Rover Home Page. July 3, 1997. http://www.jpl.nasa.gov/rover/mission.html (July 2, 1998).

Creating a while background:

1. Click the "Page Attributes" button.

2. Click "Pick" to the right of the "Color" entry in the "Background" section.
3. On the color pallette click the white color square and then click "OK".
4. Click "OK" again.

Superscript & Hyperlink to the citation below:

The "Anchor" in the Citation must be Established first.

1. Use the mouse to highlight the "2".
2. Pull down the "Format" menu, select "Type Style" and then select "Superscript".
3. Click the "Link" button while the "2" is still highlighted.
4. In the "Append Anchor Name" box enter the anchor name for the second citation.
5. Click "OK".

Create a link to external web pages:

1. Highlight the text that will link to the page.
2. Click the "Link" button.
3. In the "Link to Page" text box, type the target URL.
4. Click "OK".

Create a Table:

1. This table has 5 rows and 2 columns.
2. Put the cursor in the position of the table.
3. Click the "Create Table" button.
4. File in "5" for rows and "2" for columns.
5. Enter "0" for border size.
   This will cause the table borders To disappear
6. Click "OK".
7. Fill in the table cells with information.

Web sites that "Work for You"

The World Wide Web provides brand new and powerful opportunities for facilitating communication and educating people. Yet, most web pages (even many professionally created commercial web pages) are little more than billboards on the "Information Highway." It is important to understand the potentials of publishing on the web. Electronic communication through the World Wide Web is fundamentally different from publishing in print. People read in a different way when they read text from a computer screen. They use different tools to scan and search information. People are usually in a different frame of mind when sit at a computer compared to curling up in front of a fire with a good book. These are just a few things that a web builder must consider when setting out to design a web page. They are also issues that you can leverage to communicate better -- to help your information customers help you do your job.

What Kinds of Web Pages are Educators Building

We are passing generations of knowledge on to next generation, preparing our students to inherit their futures, and all of this within a society that is mobile, complex, and increasingly diverse. The information must flow!

At least half of the workshops that I teach today involve helping educators learn to build web pages. Conference sessions related to web building and web design are certainly the biggest draw. This originally concerned me, because establishing a school web site to satisfy the principal, or the PTA, or because the central office was requiring one seemed less important than teachers learning to skillfully use the Internet as a powerful teaching and learning tool.

Yet, I continued to work with teachers, enjoying their natural creativity. I explored the web work done by educators across the country and beyond. As a result, it has become increasingly obvious that publishing on the web, establishing effective communication venues between our information customers and ourselves helps us do our jobs. Education is an information-intensive endeavor -- perhaps our greatest. We are passing generations of knowledge on to next generation, preparing our students to inherit their futures, and all of this within a society that is mobile, complex, and increasingly diverse. The information must flow!

There are four logical types of web sites that educators are creating today. Each has its own style, goal, and objective. These types are:

- School District Web Sites,

- School Building Web Sites,

- Classroom Web Sites, and

- Project Web Sites.

School District Web Sites

The district web site will be the most formal and political in nature. Its goal is to support the broader community by:

- Making its citizens aware of general policies and standards,

- Providing a conduit through which the community can become aware of state and national policies and standards,

- Featuring programs that the district offers for students with special needs and desires,

- Instilling an impression that the school district is successfully educating its students to the standards of the community, and

- Attracting new and productive residents to the community.

There are many more goals that a district web site might have, depending on its characteristics. But the style of the design, content, and flow will be of a more professional and polished nature. The district site, of the four mentioned above, is the most likely to be implemented by professional web designers. This, of course, will be a greater likelihood of larger urban districts.

It is important to note that a district web site must facilitate communication, not just broadcast information. Knowing the community is essential to any successful school district, and a web site can effectively facilitate this communication.

Any district web site should include a fill out form for the community. But this form should be designed to invite comments and suggestions that will be of the greatest help to the district. Great care must be given to designing a form that gets the most benefit from the minute that your citizen spends filling in his information. The form should also be designed to get the information to the right person. A drop down menu could be employed so that the person filling the form can select the person to receive it. Or you might have all entries e-mailed to the central office receptionist, who is already practiced at getting information to the right person.

Also, take steps to assure that your web site is being used by a broad range of people, not just those who have Internet access at home or work. Convince the public libraries or other venues with Internet access to place the district's web site on it bookmarks, or as a link on its home page. Print a sign to post near these computers advertising the fact that people can access their school district through these computers. Do everything that you can to avoid information inequities in your community.

School Building Web Sites

The school web site serves a slightly different customer with similar and different objectives in mind. Typically, the audience is the parents, potential parents, and local community of the school. There is a tendency to consider students a customer of the school web site by creating a page of links for the students. However, students are in our schools to learn, and they learn best under the leadership of their teachers. Educational resources intended for students should be made available to them through their teacher and their classroom web sites.

The school site is designed to help parents help the school. I was recently working with an elementary school that had the problem of too many volunteers. Now we all know that an elementary school can't have too many volunteers, but managing their movements and assignments had become a time consuming task for the professionals of the school. The solution that we invented was a web form that teachers could fill out when they had specific tasks for volunteers to perform. These tasks, along with the contact information for the teacher were published as a report on a web page. When volunteers wanted to come to the school to help, they would check this web page, select a task that they were best suited for, and then report through the office and directly to the classroom or lab and to the professional who would supervise them.

Each school has its own needs. Each school has its own culture. The school's web site should be a reflection of that culture. When parents or community members have visited your school's site, they should have a sense of having visited the school itself. A school web site should be designed to be effective, but not necessarily to be professional and polished in the same way that a district site would aspire to.

One of the unique benefits of building a school web site is that your school is full of technology savvy people who, by nature of their presence, need to learn to communicate. Have students do as much of the work as possible. They can do much of the graphics, some of the copy as part of their regular classes and probably all of the coding on the side.

There is much that should be posted on a school web site. A unique and potent opportunity is to use your school's web site to help the public appreciate the teaching profession. It is easy to clearly illustrate the high standards that any teacher must meet and the impressive accomplishments that most have achieved. A school web site should advertise the fact that:

- 54% of its teachers hold a graduate degree,

- that 43% have taught for more than 15 years,

- that 26% have traveled abroad, or

- that Ms. Velez traveled to southwestern Colorado this summer to make her own slides of Neolithic Anasazi villages and relics for use in her social students classes this year.

We should use the web to promote the profession.

Classroom Web Sites

There are probably fewer classroom web sites than the previous two, but they are certainly the fastest growing, with the greatest potential for growth. They also have the greatest potential for impacting student learning.

Most frequently, teachers post web links for their students. They include general links that are regularly used by students, such as links to search engines. I examined a web site recently where a chemistry teacher had links on his classroom web site to the various lab report sheets that his students used. When a team of students needed a tessellation report sheet, they just went to the lab's computer, accessed that page through the classroom web site and printed it. This freed the teacher to spend more time supervising student learning.

Most links, however, should be presented within the context of what the students are doing in class. You should establish a list of links that are appropriate for the current unit of study, and make it available to the students. When a new unit comes up, post a new list of links. If you are posting your assignment and projects on the web site, post the links within the assignment so that students know why this link is there and how it is to be used. This is an essential way to assure the appropriate use of the Internet -- to proactively lead students into appropriate uses with clear guidance on what they are to do.

The big talk right now over the Internet is web-based learning. Usually the context is distance learning, creating web classes that people can attend remotely. The techniques that educators are employing in their web classes might also be utilized very effectively in face to face classes.

I recently corresponded with a teacher in a school in Manhattan. They were doing just this, leveraging the technology that is being developed for distance learning for their classroom students. For instance, as he covers concepts in economics, he posts questions and problems on an online discussion form for his students to respond to. Students spend two or three of their class periods a week in the computer lab where they respond to the teacher's post -

- and to each other's. The teacher reported that this style of discussion had important advantages over verbal classroom discussions since the students were able to take time to reflect on the issues and craft their responses using word processing functions. An additional advantage was the fact that the entire discussion could be archived and printed as a study resource.

I have also had teachers tell me that students who discussed class issues online, through web forums or mailing lists, typically wrote better essay answers on their tests. They had become more fluent in discussing the issues since they had been forced to reflect on the ideas and craft their ideas.

WebQuest is another tool that can easily be incorporated into a classroom web site. WebQuests are highly developed assignments for students that involve each of the following components:

1. Introduction -- sets the stage

2. Task -- what the students will be doing

3. Information sources -- a list of information resources, both networked and traditional

4. Process -- clearly described steps for what the students will be doing

5. Guidance -- on how to process and organize the information that the students have collected

6. Conclusion -- reminds the students what they have learned in the quest.

WebQuests make a logical addition to a classroom web site with forms and forums included so that the students actually work through the web in researching, building, and publishing their results. You can learn much more about WebQuest from Bernie Dodge, the inventor of the WebQuest and Tom March, one of its chief developers at:

http://edweb.sdsu.edu/webquest/webquest.html

Project Web Sites

This type of web site is not, at this time, very common. They are mostly built by organizations who have among their missions to assist schools in facilitating project based learning. The **Global SchoolNet Foundation** (http://www.gsn.org) is a prime example. Their projects are all web based. You can see excellent examples at:

http://www.gsn.org/project/

There are two important reasons why online projects should be web-based.

1. The interactive nature of the web enables context to be created for the project. The information can be organized in a way that keeps the project, its real world application, and the learning objects connected.

2. The web helps to facilitate the project. It manages the information, freeing the teacher to monitor and support student learning.

The first online projects were e-mail projects. A teacher would organize a project sequence, write an announcement e-mail message tailored to convince other classrooms to participate, and then manage the processing and flow of information manually. She also relied on other teachers to find and create context resources for their students to use in their participation.

The information and communication were linear. First the announcement, then the initial correspondence, then the work and exchange of information, and finally the conclusion. In contrast, using the web to manage your project affords you the ability to include all of the information and correspondence in one place. Participating teachers have ready access to the complete listing of information and the managing teacher can easily add and adapt the information to specific needs and situations.

The web can also be used to assist in managing the project. Many projects involve collecting information through surveys.

Traditionally, these projects were done through e-mail where survey questions were e-mailed out to classes across the country, and the results were e-mailed back. One problem with this was that the teacher had to spend a great deal of time dealing with the variety of formats people used in recording their results. Some separated the data with commas, others with returns, some put several returns between lines. Each e-mail message had to be processed differently.

If the survey data is collected through a web form, and the form e-mails the data to the teacher, then every message will be formatted the same, saving the teacher an enormous amount of time. Web forms can easily be established as explained later in this chapter.

Increasing in sophistication, a database can be employed to collect the data through a web form. Once the information is in a database, it can be reported in a wide variety of ways. These and other techniques can be used in a web project that frees the teacher to pay attention to student needs instead of managing the project.

The next part of this book will discuss some of these potentials and techniques for realizing many of them, techniques that are well within the reach of most schools.

Planning Your Web site

Perhaps the most critical step in building a web presence and the most often neglected one is planning. To build a web site that accomplishes something for you or your school requires planning. Before you start thinking about HTML coding, images to be used in the web page, or any of the information, you must plan for what you want to accomplish and how to set about that task.

Who Should be Involved in the Planning?

This is a difficult question to answer. Your planning team depends so much on the character and culture of your school or school district. The number of participants is also critical. The smaller the number, the faster you will be able to move. At the same time, critical people can easily be left out, people who can be instrumental in helping plan a more successful web presence.

Some of the people you might consider in planning a school or district site are:

- School administrators
- Media Specialist

- Representatives of Each Grade Level or Department
- Representatives from the PTA or PTO

- Technology Savvy Students
- Technology Savvy Parents

- Representation from the Central Office (communications officer and/or technology director)
- Clerical and other Support Staff

What is the Planning Process?

It is important to structure you planning session(s) as much as possible. Otherwise, the meetings can deteriorate into issues that are not particularly relevant to the construction of your school web site. Below are some questions to be answered in the planning process. These questions can serve as a structure for your meetings binding the discussions to the task at hand.

1. **Who is the intended audience of your web site?**

   Who are your stakeholders?

   - Parents,
   - the broader community,
   - people who are considering moving to your community,
   - the central office,
   - local and distant political officials

   are a few examples.

   Think also about your audience in terms of how to best design your web site. What is their reading level? What kind of access to the Internet do they have? Will they have high speed or low speed access? Are they beginners or sophisticated users? Each of these answers will guide you in the types of features you will include in your site.

2. **What are your goals and objectives?**

The distinction between goals and objectives is obscure for most people. But it is one that educators understand, almost instinctively. The goals are yours -- what you want to accomplish with your school web site. Examples include:

- Moving your school into the information age

- Improving effectiveness of teachers through communication

- Expanding the school community

- Increasing the number and effectiveness of volunteers

- Establishing online mentors for students and teachers

As teachers, our objectives describe what we want our students to know or to be able to do as a result of our instruction. As web planners, our objectives describe how we want to affect the behavior of the people, our school's stockholders, who read our web site. When thinking about these issues, it is important to identify how your parents, general community, central office, and others can help you do your job. This will point to your objectives. Examples include:

- The community develops a positive and enthusiastic impression of your school

- Parents want to become more involved in their children's learning

- The electorate is eager to support progressive schooling

- Government officials are willing to fund progressive initiatives

- Students are more engaged by their learning

Your goals and objectives are the most critical factor in building a web site that works for you. Unless you have clear ideas of what you want to accomplish, it will be difficult to build a site that accomplishes anything.

Your goals and objectives are your guidelines when selecting the features to include in your web site and also the look and feel of the site. All decisions about design should be made while looking through the lens of your goals and objectives.

3. **What information do you already have that will help you accomplish your goals?**

   This can be the most creative and exciting part of the planning process and is well suited for brainstorming. Simply list your goals and objectives, and then ask for ideas of information that will accomplish those goals.

   In considering information to be included in your web site, it is important to discuss the procedures that will be necessary to convert the information to web format (HTML). There are two ways to think about this.

   a. What will it take to convert the information to web format? If the school secretary is typing up (with a typewriter) a monthly newsletter that you would like to include on the web, then get him or her a computer with word processing software that will easily convert files to HTML.

   b. How should the information present itself? Understand that getting information onto the web is easy compared to getting the information from the user's screen into his or her understanding. Laying out information so that it presents itself effectively for accomplishing your goals is perhaps the most challenging part of creating a web site. Think about how you best understand information. Typically, people understand a picture better than prose, graphs better than tabular data, charts better than outlines.

4. **How will you structure your web site?**

   The important thing to understand about the World Wide Web is the fact that it presents information from a three-dimensional information environment. From any one point, we can go in a variety of directions depending on our information needs.

   Designing your web site's structure should take this fact into consideration. Who will your audience be? What problems are they likely to be trying to solve by coming to your web site? Where can you put the answers so that he or she can reach them with the fewest number of mouse clicks?

Always consider your goals and your audience, and the reasons that they have come to your web site. Arrange your information and links for ease, convenience, and speed.

5. **Facilitate review and feedback**

It is easy to provide e-mail links in your web page so that people can e-mail the webmaster with complaints and suggestions.

```
<a href="mailto:david@landmark-project.com">Webmaster</a>
```

Users of your web site, however, will seldom use this feature. They have come to your site to access information, not to provide it. You must be more proactive in pursuing valuable input from your web customers and here are some ideas for how to get it.

a. Teachers, as they participate in parent conference, can ask parents if they have used the web site before, what information they were looking for, if they found the information, did they enjoy the experience?

b. If your school has an end of the year survey for parents, include some questions about your web site.

c. Include a form on your web site that asks for input from users. The form should be short. It should look like a person could complete it within one minute. If it looks like it will require more investment of time that one minute, then people will not answer the questions. The form should not ask more than four questions. If you have more than four questions, then cycle them through each week. Ask four questions one week, then four different questions the next week.

d. Ask parents during PTA meetings to raise their hands if they have used the web site. Ask them to raise their hands if they found the information they were looking for. Ask them to meet with the webmaster after the meeting if they have any suggestions on how to improve the service.

e. Establish a school web site advisory council, asking members to provide feedback on the effectiveness of the web information and on its design.

Design Issues

In the Information Age, it is information that will compete for attention, in the same way that products on store shelves competed for attention in the industrial age.

Getting information coded, onto a web server, and across tens of thousands of miles of Internet is easy. The hard part is designing the pages so that the information travels the 18 inches from the reader's screen into their understanding. This involves far more than writing coherent sentences and paragraphs. It involves how the information looks, and how it is laid out. I also involves how it makes the reader's eyes move. For instance, centered text is difficult to read because it forces the reader to search and find the beginning of each line.

In the Information Age, it is information that will compete for attention, in the same way that products on store shelves competed for attention in the industrial age. Your information with accomplish this by being

- Inviting,
- Easy to scan, and
- Easy to understand

Here are a few tips for designing your web pages.

1. Goals, Goals, Goals

Always consider your goals and objectives first. Also consider them last. Anything that you can do in the design of your web pages that helps you accomplish your goals is good design. What you want to accomplish with your web site will always outweigh the rest of these suggestions.

2. Use images deliberately

In the information age, information is the commodity, and the currency is time. People are seeking information and they are paying for it with their time. Text takes very little time to load through the Internet. Images, on the other hand, take a great deal of time. If an image does not help you accomplish your goals, then do not use it. This is not to say that your web pages should have not images at all. Certainly, one of your goals is to project an image of professionalism. Be sparing with your images.

It is important to note that the file type of your image has a lot to do with its size and the amount of time it takes to load through the Internet. The two image file types that are compatible with the web are GIF *(Graphics Interchange Format)* and JPEG *(Joint*

Photographic Experts Group). Some images produce small files when saved as GIF, while other are smaller when saved as JPEG. For instance, the picture of a school house on the right, drawn with a graphics program, is 10 kilobytes in size when saved as a JPEG file, and only 4 kilobytes when saved as GIF. On the other hand, images that have higher resolution, more colors, i.e., scanned photographs or pictures taken with a digital camera will produce smaller files when saved as JPEG.

4.   Use white space

Don't think of white space as an absence of content. Use white space to draw attention to content. If you have a block of information that you want the viewer's eye to be drawn to, place a buffer of white space around it. If there is a bulleted list on a page that is of special importance to your web customers, place white space in from of the bullets.

Carefully placed white space can also give a web page a polished and professional look. Along with small and well designed images, white space can be used to give a web page a graphic intensive look, without taking a minute and a half to load.

5.   Information layout and presentation -- design for scanning

Most people do not come to the Internet to read. They come to the Internet to learn. If they want to read, they curl up by a fire with a good book.

Most people do not come to the Internet to read. They come to the Internet to learn.

People scan web pages rather than read them from top to bottom. They are usually looking for information. This is why you should design your pages for scanning. Identify text that your web customers might be looking for and bold the text, or color it, or make it a different size. You want to distinguish the text from the surrounding information so that it will draw the scanning eye. You want to create eye magnets on your page.

Using hanging indents is one way to design for scanning. Headings and subheadings should be bold, perhaps larger, but also justified to the left of the screen (headings should not be centered). The text or content beneath the headings should be indented. This way, the person who is scanning your page can easily pick up the headings to the left and then shift over to the content when they find something interesting.

6. **Menu size**

Try to keep your page menus to less than seven items. People are less likely to read a long menu, preventing them for visiting any of the valuable links from your page. If menus offer fewer than seven options, then people are more likely to read them and to link to the information that will help them solve their problem.

If you need to have more than six options from a single page then have more than one menu listing. Select the most important options, the ones that would be most relevant to most of your readers, and make them a main menu with large and bold text, and attention grabbing bullets. This is the menu that would draw the readers eye. Then if they see value in your web site from this main menu, then their eyes will wonder to other less attracting menu listings.

7. **Page size**

Working a mouse is work. The less you make people use their mouse, the happier they are and the more positively they take your information. This requires that you make lots of decisions regarding page size. Your choices frequently are having a long web page that forces the reader to use his or her mouse to scroll endlessly down the page, or having lots of short pages, requiring the reader to continue to click options from a menu.

Usually it is preferable to have smaller pages. They are easier to manage for the reader and give a greater sense of organization. However there are two very good reasons to go with longer pages. If the nature of the information and its use might cause the reader to scan the page for occurrences of specific words or phrases, then the long page has an advantage. The reader can use the Find feature that is in most browsers to search the entire contents of the page for the word or phrase.

Another advantage of longer pages is the ability to print them. If the information is such that people would want to have a printed copy, then they can print the single long page once. If the information is divided into several shorter pages, then the user will have to print many times to get all of the information.

Another important consideration is the fact that most people do not scroll down a web page...at all. Their decision to scroll depends on what they see at the top of the page. Therefore, the top six inches of your web page is the most crucial part. This is where you place your hook. This is where you advertise the information, convincing the reader that he or she should want to scroll further.

Making Your School Web Site Interactive

The web, by nature, is interactive. The information you receive depends on where you click your mouse. This is an important distinction between the Internet and other forms of communication. With the Internet, the information consumer is in control of the information.

It is equally important to understand that the web is becoming a far more sophisticated communication medium, rapidly extending beyond simply clicking hyperlinks. The web, today, can be used not only to publish information but to collect data and to facilitate interaction between people, creating places to meet and supporting virtual communities.

The reader controls the published information by what he or she clicks. However, the World Wide Web has also become a facility for collecting information from the reader and encouraging a sense of community among your web customers.

Jeffrey Harrow, senior consulting engineer for Compaq Corporation and editor of *The Rapidly Changing Face of Computing* (http://www.compaq.com/rcfoc) said in his January 18, 1999 issue of that publication that, "1998 saw $32 billion transacted over the Internet, and that will double to $68 billion this year."[*] This indicates that people are increasingly expecting more

---

[*] Harrow , Jeffrey R. "The Rapidly Changing Face of Computing." January 18, 1999. http://www.digital.com/info/rcfoc/19990118.htm (May 29, 1999).

from a web page than just reading materials and pictures. They want to be able to do things over the Internet, and they will be expecting to do things over their children's school web site.

This section will discuss features that you can add to your web site that will make it more interactive, more useful to you and your institution, and more fun for your customers.

Forms for Collecting Information

You probably think that you need sophisticated database software and customized CGI *(Common Gateway Interface)* scripts to collect information from your readers via web forms. Until recently that was true. Today, however, there are a number of services that enable you to create web forms for your site, through which readers of your page can submit information to you.

Response-O-Matic (**http://www.response-o-matic.com/**) is one such service. Their web page provides a form through which you enter the e-mail address to which you want the submitted data sent

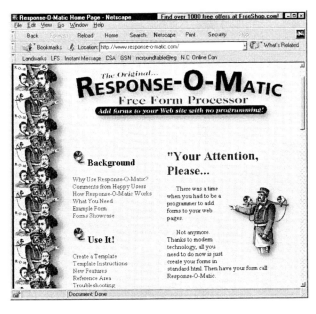

and a few other pieces of information. Then their software produces the HTML code that will create the essential parts of your form. *Response-O-Matic's* system dynamically creates the HTML code, places it in the returned web page, where you can copy and paste it into your web editor. You use your editor to add the form entry elements (text boxes, radio buttons, scrolling text windows, etc.) and further layout the page. When your web page is installed on a standard web server, input that your readers provide through the form will be e-mailed to the address that you stipulated.

As an example, we are going to build a web form for an online project called, *The Eratosthenese Project*.

The Eratosthenese Project

Eratosthenese, a Greek, who was the chief librarian of the great Library of Alexandria, was the first known person to accurately calculate the circumference of the earth. He did this by comparing the length of the shadows cast be the sun at a specific time and day in various parts of the country. He did this approximately 200 BC, 1700 years before Columbus, and missed the exact figure by only 50 miles (80 km).

This ingenious math activity was first run as an e-mail project by Al Rogers, who is now the Director of the Global SchoolNet Foundation (http://www.gsn.org). It asks students take a meter stick outside at a specific time (EST) on a specific date and to hold it straight up on a flat surface of ground. Then they are to measure the length of the shadow cast by the sun.

The classes then report their shadow lengths, and the latitude and longitude, to each other over e-mail. When the data has been collected by all classes, they begin calculating the circumference of the earth in much the way that Eratosthenese did over 2000 years ago.

We will create a form through which students can submit their Eratosthenese data.

Here are the steps for setting up a form on your web site using *Response-O-Matic*:

1. From the *Response-O-Matic* front page, click **Create a Template.**

    http://www.freedback.com

2. You will be asked to enter the following information:

    - Your e-mail address

- Your name

- The subject line for the e-mail that you receive

- The title you want to appear at the top of the thank you page (this is the page that will appear when your web visitor has pressed the submit button).

- The return link URL (the page that you want your web visitor to return to from the Submit page).

- The name of the return link

You are finally asked to select background text colors for the page that your web visitor will go to when they click the submit button.

3. After a moment a page will appear with instructions and the code for your web form page. Copy the code, then run a web editor.

4. For our example, we will use AOLPress. Run the program, start a new file, and then click the **Show HTML** button to switch to their raw code mode. Then delete out the page code that AOLPress automatically includes in a page, and paste in the code that you copied from *Response-O-Matic*. Finally, switch back to the edit mode to see the page created by our form service.

5. *Response-O-Matic* creates:

- A text box for the visitor's name,

- A text box for their e-mail address,

- Four radio buttons,

- Four check boxes,

- A drop down menu,

- A scrolling text window, and

- Submit and reset buttons.

It is important to note that most people will not fill out a form that looks like it takes more than a minute to complete. You should design your form to get the best information out of that one-minute interview.

You are welcome to use these information entry elements. However, creating your own give you more flexibility in designing your form. It is important to note that most people will not fill out a form that looks like it takes more than a minute to complete. You should design your form to get the best information out of that one-minute interview.

The essential elements to keep are the e-mail text box and the submit and reset buttons. They are all critical to the successful operation of the form. You can delete the rest.

There is an HTML form reference section on page 194. But this is probably a good time to dissect the typical input form tag.

The Input Form Tag

There are a variety of input form tags that produce elements on web pages for people to submit information into the web page. A majority of elements are produced by the <input> tag. However, others include the <select></select> and <texteara></textarea> tags, which have beginning and ending parts.

What these tags have in common are their attributes. Here is a typical input tag.

<input type="radio" name="gender" value="male">

(Continued)

(Continued from previous page)

Here are descriptions of the most common attributes:

Type -- The type attribute is used with the input tags to tell what type of entry element you want to produce. Text, radio, and checkbox are only three, and they produce a single line text box, radio button, and check box respectively.

Name -- The name attribute identifies the information that the visitor is submitting. It labels the information so that the person or computer software that receives it knows what the information is or where it goes.

Value -- Value indicates the information that is to be carried by the name by default. In other words, if a single line text box has a value of "New York, NY", then if the visitor does not enter a city, "New York, NY" will be carried as the default. Value tags are required for radio buttons and check boxes. The *value* is carried if these buttons are checked true.

6. After having deleted out all elements except for the e-mail and the submit and reset buttons, you will need to identify the elements that you need to add. For the Eratosthenese Project we will need:

- Teacher's Name
- School
- E-mail Address
- Latitude -- degrees, minutes, direction from Equator

- Longitude -- degrees, minutes, direction from Prime Meridian
- Shadow cast by the sun

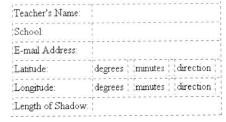

7. In order to organize the form and make it easy to read for the web visitor, we will use AOLPress' table tools to create this table and content.

8. Next you use the form tool box from AOLPress to insert the appropriate entry elements.

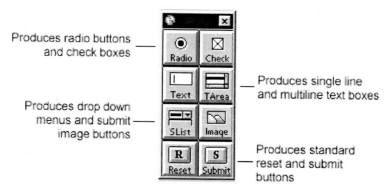

Produces radio buttons and check boxes

Produces drop down menus and submit image buttons

Produces single line and multiline text boxes

Produces standard reset and submit buttons

You will produce single line text boxes for all of the elements except for the direction from the Equator and the Prime Meridian. For these you will use drop down menus. Also, be sure to move the existing e-mail text box into the correct table cell since the e-mail text will produce a reply-to e-mail address when the data is delivered. Here are the results.

Teacher's Name:					
School:					
E-mail Address:					
Latitude:	degrees	minutes	direction	North	
Longitude:	degrees	minutes	direction	West	
Length of Shadow:					

It is important to note that the "name" attributes that are entered are logical -- names that you will recognize when the data is e-mailed to your e-mail address.

7. Finally, complete the rest of your web page, save it, and upload the page to a web server. Your Eratosthenese project web page might end our looking like this.

❊ **Response-O-Matic Form - Netscape**   NetSonic Pro Sale $19.95 (50% OFF) - Ends SUNDAY!   ▫ ◻ ✕

File   Edit   View   Go   Window   Help

Back   Forward   Reload   Home   Search   Netscape   Print   Security   Stop   ▮

Bookmarks   Location: file:///C|/Presentations/T E X T S/eratosthenes/index.html   ▾   What's Related

Landmarks   LFS   Instant Message   CSA   GSN   ncroundtable@eg   N.C. Online Con

ERATOSTHENESE PROJECT

Introduction

On October 15th, at exactly 12:00 noon, Easter Standard Time, we are going back 3,000 years to the time of Eratosthenese. Here we will use trigonometry to calculate the circumference of the earth. To register send an e-mail message with your name, name of school, grade, and subject to:

sjohnson@sms.k12.mn.us

Instructions:

On October 15th, 12:00 noon, go to a flat and unshaded area of your school campus with a meter stick. Hold the meter stick straight up, perpendicular to the ground, and then measure the length of the shadow cast by the sun in inches. Then record your finding on the form to the right including your map coordinates and the length of the shadow.

By registering for this project, you will receive all finding of for the locations of each participant as an e-mail message.

Who was Eratosthenese?

Eratosthenese was born in Greece and became the chief librarian of the Library at Alexandria Egypt, the greates depository of books in the pre-Roman world. It is famous, though, for successfully calculated the circumference of the earth over 1,200 years before Christopher Columbus.

Teacher's Name: [   ]

School: [   ]

E-mail Address: [   ]

Latitude: degrees [   ]   minutes [   ]   direction [North ▾]

Longitude: degrees [   ]   minutes [   ]   direction [West ▾]

Length of Shadow: [   ]

[Submit]   [Reset]

Document: Done

Here is a sample e-mail message that holds the information submitted by a participant in the project.

Other Applications

Here are a few ways that educators might use web forms.

1. Create feedback forms for your **school's web site** so that readers might provide **comments and suggestions** about your page.

2. You might use these forms as a way for having **students turn in their assignments**. This would be especially useful for distance learning or web-based courses.

3. **Online auctions as a fundraiser.** Many schools hold silent auctions for items donated by the PTA. Using web forms, you could move your auction to the web and run it year round.

4. Create a form for your teachers designed to input each day's **homework assignments**. Then have the information sent to a mailing list of parents who have requested that they get the homework assignments for their children.

5. **Organize an online literary magazine** for the schools in your district or with other schools around the world. You can create a web form for other schools to use to send you their original literary works.

6. Create **opinion polls** for other students or for the community. Then analyze the results as a mathematics or social studies project.

Here are descriptions of HTML form tags:

Tag	Common Attributes		Special Attributes
	Name Labels the information	**Value** Defines the default value	
FORM	The FORM tag defines the entire form. It describes where the entered content will be sent when the SUBMIT button is pressed. It also defines how the information will be structured.		
			ACTION describes where the entered content will be sent (usually a URL) METHOD describes how the entered content should be formatted (either GET or POST)
	Example: <FORM METHOD="get" ACTION="http://sample.com/bin/process.cgi">		
INPUT	The <INPUT> tag displays devices that the reader of a web page can use to submit information.		
	X	X The content of the VALUE attribute will appear in the textbox for TEXT type INPUTs.	**SIZE** defines the width of TEXT type inputs. **MAXLENGTH** defines the maximum number of characters that can be entered. **TYPE** Describes the kind of input device to be displayed. Types include:
		TEXT **HIDDEN** **RADIO** **CHECKBOX** **RESET** **SUBMIT**	(a standard, one line text box), (no input device at all. The information in the **VALUE** attribute is automatically delivered), (displays a radio button. If it is clicked on, then the information in the **VALUE** attribute is delivered), (displays a check box. If it is check true, then the information in the value attribute is delivered), (displays a reset button which sets all of the input fields to their default), (displays a submit button that sends to its destination, all of the information that has been entered into the form)
	Example: <INPUT TYPE=text VALUE="yes" NAME="answer"> From this tag, a text box will be displayed with the word "yes" automatically appearing in the box (the user can replace "yes" with another answer). When the submit button is clicked, the information is sent to its destination.		

Tag	Common Attributes		Special Attributes
	Name Labels the information	**Value** Defines the default value	
TEXTAREA	The **TEXTAREA** tag displays a larger text box within which several lines of text can be entered.		
	X		**WRAP** This indicates whether the text entered into the box will word wrap. PHYSICAL or VIRTUAL indicates that it will wrap. OFF indicates that it will not wrap.
	Example: <TEXTAREA COLS=30 ROWS=3 NAME="x"> </TEXTAREA> Note:Text that is entered into the HTML file between the beginning and ending **TEXTAREA** tags will appear in the multi-line text box.		
SELECT **&** **OPTION**	The **SELECT** tags define dropdown and scrolling menus. One **OPTION** tag is necessary for each option in the menu.		
	X	X The value can be set on OPTION tags when the value to be carried is different from the OPTION prompt.	**SIZE** If the size is one (1), then the code will produce a drop down menu. If the size equals the number of items or options, then a menu window will be produced. If the size is more than 1 but less than the number of options, then a scrolling menu window will be displayed. **MULTIPLE** If the word MULTIPLE is included in the SELECT tag, then users will be able to select multiple options.
	Example: <SELECT NAME="choice" SIZE=3> <OPTION VALUE=A>Dog <OPTION VALUE=B>Cat <OPTION VALUE=C>Hamster <OPTION VALUE=D>Lizzard </SELECTED>		

Here are some URLs of free form services on the web:

Service	URL
FreeForm An free form service that e-mails input to a predetermined e-mail address.	http://www.note.com/success/public/freeform/
Bravenet.com Bravenet offers free e-mail forms and many other web-based services.	http://www.bravenet.com
Survey9 Interactive Survey Creator This services allows you to create and track surveys on your web site.	http://www.survey9.com/
WWW Survey Builder Here is another online survey creator.	http://mail.infotrieve.com/isurvey/
AnyForm This is another form service that e-mails results. You can download and use their CGI on your server or use theirs.	http://mail.infotrieve.com/isurvey/
Free-Mail This is a mail service that allow you to create e-mail forms on your web page. It eliminates the need to use the "mailto:" tag.	http://www.remote-software.com/free.mail.html
Form Mail This is a customizable services that processes and organizes mail forms from your web page.	http://www.vpdev.com/freestuff/help/formmail.shtml

Other community-building services on the Internet

Service	URL
CHAT	
It is important to note that chat rooms are notorious for attracting people who will try to disrupt conversation with unsavory comments. When establishing chat rooms for students to use, it would be wise to have them scheduled and to have a teacher or other adult in the room to monitor the conversations.	
Irc.ramlink.net This chat service can be accessed from the web or standard chat clients such as mIRC (http://www.mirc.com/). The service also allows webmasters to set up a chat room directly on their web site.	http://irc.ram-page.com/
CrZyChat This is a Java script chat service that you can add to your web site.	http://www.crzy.com/
MultiChat This is a free Java-based chat room. It can be installed and set-up on web sites. You can also link your site's chat room to thousands of others.	http://www.multisoftcorp.com/
SneakerChat.com Another service that allows you to set up a chat room on your web site.	http://sneakerchat.com/
ParaChat Just fill out a form, copy some lines of HTML, paste them into your web page and you have chat.	http://www.parachat.com/
Beseen.com Another service for offering chat from your web site.	http://beseen.com/
SITE COUNTERS AND TRACKERS	
SuperStats This is an excellent service that provides a detailed report on the hits, the rate of hits through the day, referring web sites, and	http://www.superstats.com/

Service	URL
domains of your web customers.	
Better Counter Another counter that provides detailed reports to better track the usage of your web site. http://tracker.clicktrade.com/tracker/tracker.dll?to='http://www.better-counter.com/'&ad=55774&lp=40720	
TheCounter.com Another counter with reports on the usage of your web site.	http://www.thecounter.com/
ShowStat Statistics A quality report generating service. It includes the countries that have visited your site.	http://www.showstat.com/
StarCounter This one offers many styles for the text of your counter.	http://www.aswp.com/starcounter/
GUESTBOOKS	
Phaistos Guestbooks This is a completely customizable guestbook service.	http://phaistos.forthnet.gr/services/guestbooks/
Bravenet.com Another fully customizable guestbook.	http://www.bravenet.com/
Alx Guestbook Service This unique services offers message censoring, appearance control, easy font settings, etc.	http://www.alxbook.com/
GuestWorld This is a large and popular service that has recently added some new features including visitors stats and a form that lets you simultaneously E-mail everyone who's signed your guestbook.	http://www.lpage.com/

Note: Many of the services described in this chapter may not work if your web server is located behind a firewall.

Building a School Web Site Without HTML

One of the most important reasons to build a school, classroom, or project web site is to facilitate community. Your school's community is an important part of its culture. It defines your school. The community determines what kind of volunteer help you get, the contributions from the PTA, and the degree and effectiveness of teacher collaboration.

A web site can also be used to extend the community of your school. As much as we urge parents to become more involved in their children's schools, the simple fact is that for many talented parents with much to contribute, their schedules make it impossible to be on the school campus when needed. However, through the web, there may be ways for these people to contribute by mentoring through e-mail, chatting with the class about their work or hobbies, or donating materials to the classrooms of their children.

Being able to build web forms and establish chat rooms is one way of facilitating this sense of community in your school. Another, and perhaps more important way for your web site to become an integral reflection of your school, is if a large number of people can publish content to your site. If teachers, staff, selected parents, and administrators can all contribute contents, images, and other information to your school's site, then it better reflects all aspects of your school's community.

There are a number of services available on the Internet that have positioned themselves to help people facilitate online communities. Perhaps the most sophisticated is Schoollife a unique service run by KOZ, Inc in Research Triangle Park, North Carolina. The concept behind this company, which was organized by the owner of the second newspaper in this country to go online (http://www.nandotimes.com/), is *community publishing*. They have created a database-driven system that enables and encourages all members of an organization to take part in publishing on their web site, as opposed to everything going through a central web master.

This arrangement has particular value to schools because of the limited time that educators have. It is unrealistic to expect teachers to author web pages. HTML should not be among the skills of every teacher in your school.

Not only is the Schoollife service dedicated to making web publishing a community activity, but its web sites also include features that facilitate community among your web visitors. These features include:

- **Online discussion forums**

- **Chat rooms**

- **Interactive calendars**

- **Feed back forms**

Each of these features can be activated with only a few button clicks.

Here are the steps for establishing a Schoollife school web site:

1. Go to the Schoollife web site at:

    http://www.schoollife.net/

2. Click, **Put your school online** from the first page. Then click the **Click Here Get Started** image to start setting up your user account.

3. Complete the web form under **Create new user account here**, and then click **Create New User** at the bottom of the page. Then read the Terms and Conditions and click **Agree to Terms** to accept them.

4. At the welcome page, click **Continue**. You will receive a web page that will allow you to create your own web site on SchoolLife. Enter at the following prompts:

Channel	This will be *K-12 Schools*
Web Site Name	A short and catchy name for your site

Web Site Description	A longer description of your site. You are limited to 255 characters.
Your Location	City, state, zip, country
Contact E-mail Address	The e-mail address of the site administrator

Click, **Create Now.**

5. From the **Congratulations** page click **You may now visit your web site's home page** at the bottom. This will deliver you to a standard Schoollife page.

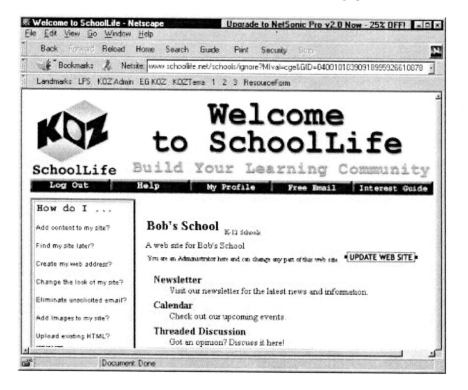

6. On this page, you will find a button called, **UPDATE WEB SITE**. You are the only person who will see this

button, unless you grant administration rights to other people. When you click this button, you will receive a web page that enables you to manage the site in a wide variety of ways. From here you can add content to the home page and to other pages in the site.

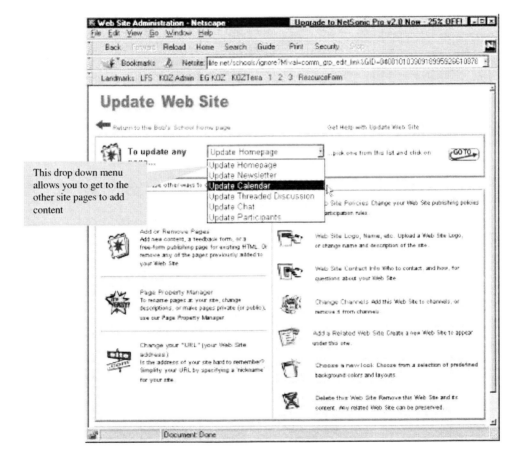

7. Also from this management page you can customize the site. Here are some of the options:

Add or Remove Pages	This option helps you add pages to your site. You can add a standard Schoollife web page, a feedback form, or a freeform publishing page. Freeform pages enable web-savvy educators to create fully

	customized pages using HTML code
	Added web pages will automatically show up on the main menu of the site's front page.
Page Property Manager	This is heart of managing your Schoollife school site. Here you can:
	▪ Determine whether the main menu should be a vertical or horizontal list and change the names of each item.
	▪ Set up a search tool so that visitors can search your site for keywords.
	▪ Activate and deactivate interactive features of your site (online discussion, chat, calendar, etc.). You can also determine if the features will be available to all visitors, or to specific people whom you have identified.
Change your "URL"	Because Schoollife is a database driven site, the addresses of the individual pages will make little sense to most people. With this option, you can set an address name or alias for your site. If we enter *bobschool* for our new site, then the URL for the site will be:
	http://www.schoollife.net/schools/bobschool
Web Site Policies	There are basically three levels of Schoollife users: site administrators, participants, and casual visitors. The site administrator can use this option to set the rights that participants and casual visitors have in your site. For instance, the chat room can be set so that only participants (for instance, students in your class and students in a class in England) can use it or even see it. The site administrator can set a page so that casual users can read it, but registered participants can update the content.
	In addition, the site administrator can set pages so that if participants update the page, the administrator

	must approve the change before it becomes public.
Web Site Logo, Name, Etc.	Here you can change the name and description of your web site. You can also upload a logo or picture of your school that will appear at the top of each page in your site.
Web Site Contact Info	You can change the contact person and e-mail address from this option.
Change Channels	Channels are categories of web sites in Schoollife and the larger KOZ community. Here you can change your channel from K-12 Schools to other categories, such as: PTA, educational resources, etc.
Add a Related Web Site	One of the uniquely powerful features of Schoollife and KOZ is the ability to spawn separate sites from an original one. From a school perspective, individual classroom sites can be spawned from the school's site, each with its own discussion forums, chat rooms, and calendar. Each spawned site also has its own site administrator.
Choose a new look	There are a wide variety of background templates that can be selected for your site. They include images and formatting for your site.
Delete this Web Site	Self-explanatory.

Here is our Bob's School web page after just a few button clicks. Now we can start adding more content, each addition selected from a large number of multimedia layouts.

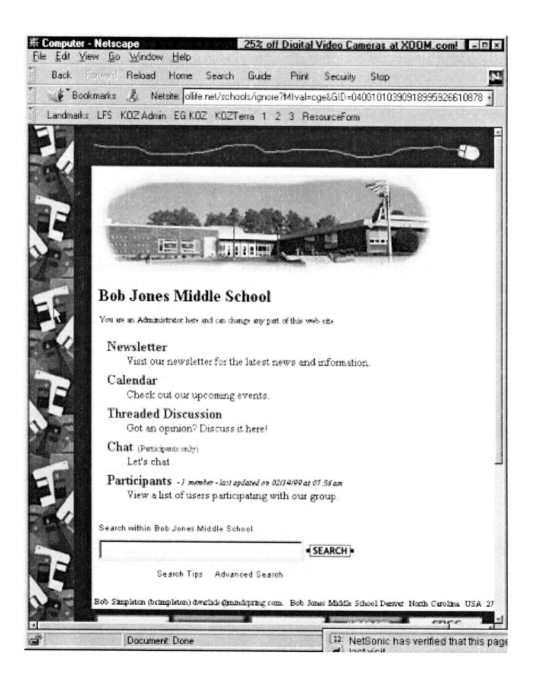

Bob Jones Middle School

You are an Administrator here and can change any part of this web site.

Newsletter
Visit our newsletter for the latest news and information.

Calendar
Check out our upcoming events.

Threaded Discussion
Got an opinion? Discuss it here!

Chat (Participants only)
Let's chat

Participants - 1 member - last updated on 02/14/99 at 07:59 am
View a list of users participating with our group.

Search within Bob Jones Middle School

Search Tips   Advanced Search

Bob Stapleton (bstapleton) dewitide@mindspring.com Bob Jones Middle School Denver North Carolina USA 27

Conclusion

I have taken you on a fairly wild ride for the last two hundred pages or so. We have explored some rather radical ideas about education. We have also learned practical techniques for finding information on the Internet, taking advantage of the digital qualities of that information, and constructing information products as teaching materials and as valuable activities for students. We have also examined issues regarding your school or school district's web site, important considerations in planning and maintaining it, and some techniques for making your site work for you.

Assuming that you agree with at least some of the ideas behind this book, what do you do next? As a teacher, how do you go about making these skills a part of your teaching arsenal? What can you do to pursue some of the goals of this book and goals that have occurred to you as you have read this book?

First of all, seek professional staff development for the other teachers in your school and school district. *My phone number and e-mail address are in the front of the book.* But far more important than that, form a community of fellow educators, set goals, learn, and share.

Here are other suggestions. You do not need to follow them in this order. You do not need to follow them exactly. But do follow up on this book by learning more about how technology can help you and your students do your jobs.

1. Find someone in your school or district who has a genuine knack for technology. It is better if he or she still speaks English as their first language, but this is not essential. You want a local resource on whom you can call for technical help. When you have identified this person:

    •   Bake him or her some cookies.

    •   Ask that person to explain HTML, FTP, TCP-IP and any other techie things that you may or may not have been curious about. Your techie will explain it because they are looking for converts.

    •   Then ask your techie to fix your printer and ask if you can watch.

2. Get a copy of your school and/or school district's technology plan and read it. Look especially for the goals of the plan. Look also at the technology strategies and any timelines regarding the implementation of those strategies. Learn where you are in the timeline. Then learn what you can about the technologies that are on their way and find out, through mailing lists, how other schools are using them. It is important to position yourself so that you can begin utilizing emerging technologies, as they become available.

3. Form that community. Talk with your teacher friends and do not limit yourself to the teachers in your school. Share with them what you have learned in this book. Buy them a copy of the book or at least give them the URL.

    http://www.landmark-project.com/RMFM/

4. Brainstorm ideas on how you might use some of the ideas in this book, and perhaps even more importantly, go beyond the book, creating new strategies. You want to

establish two or three goals. Write down descriptions for two or three things that you would like to do with the Internet and related technologies before the end of the school year, or by the beginning of the next school year.

5.   Get together regularly with your community, either in person or virtually over the Internet. Share what you have learned. Send one e-mail message to each member each week sharing something that you have learned about e-mail, or browsing the Internet, or about a search engine, or about a web site that you discovered. Require every other member to do the same.

6.   Plan collaborative projects with the other teachers in your community. Even if you teach third grade and your friend teaches high school history, collaborate! Use your imagination.

7.   Join a mailing list. Have the other members of your group join other mailing lists. Share with the group messages from your mailing list that would be of value to them.

8.   Once a week find a picture, some text, a diagram, or at least an idea from the Internet and use it in your classroom.

9.   Participate in an online project. Go to the Global School House web site and read through projects that they are coordinating. Also use their *Projects Registry* and read through proposals posted by other teachers. Plan to participate in at least two projects this year.

10. If you do not have a computer at home, buy one. If you do not have access to the Internet at home, get it. Neither of these items are inexpensive for teachers. But if you are going to learn how to use technology and the Internet, it will not happen at school. It will happen in the convenience of your home, in the quiet of the evening, in the comfort of jeans and a T-shirt.

One last thought. Stop thinking of yourself as a teacher, and start seeing yourself as a learning consultant. Your job is to help your students learn and develop skills. Sometimes this involves delivering the knowledge to them, but often they should be learning within experiences that you have crafted for them, where they are finding their own information raw materials, processing the materials into their own knowledge and building an information product from their knowledge. Also spend time sharpening your own skills and knowledge. In order to remain valuable to your students and school, you must stay on top of and just to the leading edge of the wave. Otherwise, you and your students will slide behind.

I had a learning consultant when I was a freshman in high school. His name was Bill Edwards. Like most secondary schools, we had electives. Where I grew up band members took band. If you were not in the band, you took industrial arts. This was fine. We were, after all, in the Industrial Age.

I learned a great deal in Mr. Edwards' industrial arts class. I also learned in a different way. If he had taught us Industrial Age skills the same way that I was learning most of my Information Age skills, then he would have stacked wood on my desk and told me to practice driving nails.

Instead, I learned a wide variety of industrial skills by building a kayak. Others in the class built bookshelves, stools, gun racks (I do not believe that they are building gun racks anymore in schools), and chessboards. Rather than practicing individual and unrelated skills, we learned and mastered skills as an interrelated ensemble of tools, within the context of a product that would be used and enjoyed by another person.

Mr. Edwards was my consultant. He helped me make decisions about the design and implementation of my boat. He asked me questions that made me think about what I was doing, to look at my tasks from the most productive perspectives. He also taught me proper techniques -- **BASICS**. Perhaps the most important thing that he taught me was how to work, how to manage my resources, and my time, how to set goals, and how to complete a task that would be enjoyed by others.

Thank you, Mr. Edwards!

Index